THE BEST OF
BUSINESS CARD DESIGN | 8
SIBLEY/PETEET DESIGN | AUSTIN

ROCKPORT

THE BEST OF

BUSINESS CARD DESIGN | 8

SIBLEY/PETEET DESIGN | AUSTIN

BEVERLY MASSACHUSETTS

ROCKPORT PUBLISHERS

First published in the United States of America by Rockport Publishers, a member of Quayside Publishing Group

100 Cummings Center Suite 406-L Beverly, MA 01915-6101 Telephone: (978)282.9590 Fax: (978)283.2742 www.rockpub.com

Design: Sibley/Peteet Design, Austin | Cover: Rex Peteet | Photography: Ned Witrogen | Hand Photography: Matthew Wetzler | Printed in China

Library of Congress Cataloging-in-Publication Data available | ISBN-13: 978-1-59253-575-0 | ISBN-10: 1-59253-575-5 | 10 9 8 7 6 5 4 3 2 1

This book is dedicated to all of
the designers around the world that
contributed their best work to this 8th
edition of Best of Business Card Design.
In addition we would like to thank
our friends at Rockport Publishers
for all of their tireless support.
And lastly, thanks to the terrific team
at Sibley/Peteet Design, Austin.

THE BEST OF BUSINESS CARD DESIGN

Business cards have come a long way since their predecessors first appeared in European society in the mid-1600s. These early cards, then referred to as "Visite de Biletes," or visiting cards, eventually evolved into two categories serving distinct purposes: a card used when calling on an individual or group socially, and a card that served as a small advertisement for one's trade or service. Along with their aesthetic and functional evolution, a specific protocol emerged of when and how to use the cards, format standards, proper printing and paper choice, maps (there were no street numbers, so maps were necessary), even intent or purpose. For example, there was an entire vocabulary based on calling card folding. A card folded in half meant the owner was calling on the entire family. A card's upper right corner folded down meant it was delivered personally.

These cards, and their ritual and use, found their way to America in the 1800s. These almost concurrent genres ultimately morphed into what we know today as the business card, and its use has become interchangeable whether calling socially or for business purposes. Thus a whole new category in branding one's self or business was born.

Functionally speaking, the business card has become so much more than an introduction or a method to hype your wares. Business cards tell a story; they open doors; they make a statement; they answer questions; they connect; they unlock and initiate conversation; they provide information and serve as an extension of one's self. Hence—and adverse to what you would expect in this digital age—the very low-tech business card proliferates and maintains a critical purpose in bringing people and business together around the world.

As depicted on the cover of *Best of Business Card Design 8*, we suggest metaphorically many of the things that good business cards do well. This is the criteria we used as a baseline to select the cards that were most successful at telling their individual stories, their degree of appropriateness for a particular business or individual, as well as how uniquely they distinguished themselves. As we juried, we asked ourselves: Does the card appropriately and efficiently communicate? Is the information easily accessible? Is it innovative in the genre? Overdone? Is it practical? (We gave wide berth here, and measured by the necessity to concept, and allowed real creativity to trump mass production feasibility.) Or did we just think it was cool, and wish we had done it?

After reviewing thousands of entries from more than 25 countries, we selected close to 400 of the very best. We saw a lot of laser die cuts, cards with silkscreen on Plexiglas, applied stickers that wrap, embossing, sewing, folding, punching, foiling, and elaborate printing on both sides. By contrast, we also saw the very restrained and elegant. Here you will discover extraordinary examples of each. We hope you are inspired by this eighth edition, giving you another bi-annual snapshot of how the world is connecting itself, and a closer look at how far the visiting card has come since that first introduction more than 350 years ago.

1

2

PATTI MODELLI

NEW YORK

VERONIQUE IMPERIAL

TEL 646.872.3153
PATTIMODELLI@VERIZON.NET

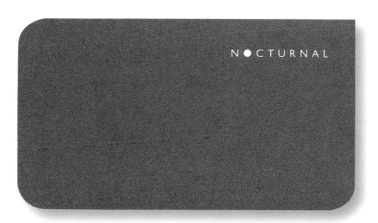

N●CTURNAL

3

Hello. For your safety and well being, this unique business card has been thoughtfully designed with three rounded corners. While we're unaware of any conclusive research regarding business-card-related injuries, we feel it stands to reason that a business card with three rounded corners is at least 75% safer than your average card. (Sure, we could have rounded all four corners, but what would life be without a little risk?) We hope this attention to detail fosters good will and communicates our commitment to intelligent design. When you think about it, this card neatly sums up what it is that we do best: Look out for our clients' interests by creating good will through intelligent communication and design that's always well rounded and sometimes a little edgy. That's us, Nocturnal Graphic Design Studio.
Ken Peters, Creative Director ken@nocturnaldesign.com ph: 480.688.4207
View samples from our portfolio at www.nocturnaldesign.com

BARRON LAU
CEO | CREATIVE DIRECTOR

E-MAIL: BARRONL@PRESSURE.ORG
BLACKBERRY PIN: 30075CCE
MOBILE: 416-805-8002
IM: BARRONL@PRESSURE.ORG

2820 14TH AVE., SUITE 101
MARKHAM, ONTARIO
L3R 0S9
PHONE: 905-305-0979 x11
FAX: 905-305-0415
WWW.PRESSURE.ORG

1

1

design firm: Pressure
art director: Jun Woo
designer: Vasilios Goulopoulos
client: Pressure
software/hardware: Adobe Illustrator CS2

2

design firm: Design Ranch
art director: Michelle Sonderegger and Igred Sidie
designer: Tad Carpenter and Rachel Karaca
client: Nara

3

design firm: W Design
art director: Kristy Weyhrich
designer: Kristy Weyhrich
client: W Design
software/hardware: Adobe Illustrator and Quark Xpress

Eddie Lauth

◆

485 Scenery Drive

State College, PA 16801

United States

◆

814.234.2903

eddie@frenchleaveresort.com

1

FRENCH LEAVE

2

Mindd Foundation
PO Box 151 Vaucluse
NSW 2030 Australia
T +61 2 9388 7383
www.mindd.org
info@mindd.org

Leslie Embersits

Metabolic
Immuno
Neurological
Digestive
Disorders

Mindd
Foundation

Mindd Foundation
PO Box 151 Vaucluse
NSW 2030 Australia
T +61 2 9388 7383
www.mindd.org
info@mindd.org

Metabolic
Immuno
Neurological
Digestive
Disorders

ASFOOR & KHATIB **TRADING GROUP**

P.O.Box: 22733 Safat 13088 Kuwait
Tel.: (+965) 57 47 374 - Fax: (+965) 57 18 476
www.aktgroup.net - tkhatib@aktgroup.net

TAREK KHATIB
DEPUTY MANAGING DIRECTOR

JOE FU 傅雲飛
(852) 9232 8206
(86) 1352 8760 066

ACME PRINTING CO. 鹽精印務公司

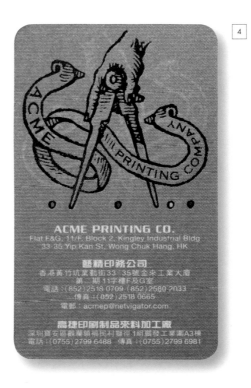

ACME PRINTING CO.
Flat F&G, 11/F, Block 2, Kingley Industrial Bldg
33-35 Yip Kan St, Wong Chuk Hang, HK

鹽精印務公司
香港黃竹坑業鹽街33-35號金光工業大廈
第二期 11字樓F及G室
電話：(852)2518 0709 (852)2580 2033
傳真：(052)2518 0665
電郵：acmep@netvigator.com

高捷印刷制品來料加工廠
深圳寶安區觀瀾鎮桂民村觀瀾 1號鹽發工業園A3棟
電話：(0755)2799 6488 傳真：(0755)2799 6981

1

design firm: Sommese Design
art director: Kristin Sommese
               and Lanny Sommese
designer: Kristin Sommese, Lanny
               Sommese, and Ryan Russell
client: Lauth Development Co.
paper/materials: Beckett Expression Radiance

2

design firm: There
art director: There
designer: There
client: Mindd Foundation
software/hardware: Adobe Illustrator
paper/materials: Various

3

design firm: Paragon Marketing
               Communications
art director: Louai Alasfahani
designer: Khalid Al-Rifae
client: Asfoor & Khatib Trading Group
software/hardware: Adobe Illustrator
paper/materials: Cache 350 gsm with lamination

4

design firm: Root Idea
art director: Ken Lee
designer: Ken Lee
illustrator: Ken Lee
client: Acme Printing
software/hardware: Photoshop and Adobe Illustrator
paper/materials: Antalis, Reaction Alpine
               Sparkling Water

1

Washington, D.C.
202.337.4112

Las Vegas, Nevada
702.364.5888

abalv.com

Todd-Avery Lenahan
PRINCIPAL & CEO

2

LOUVIERE + VANESSA

Jeff Louviere + Vanessa S. Brown
732 Mazant Street | New Orleans, Louisiana 70117
504-940-5498   louviereandvanessa.com

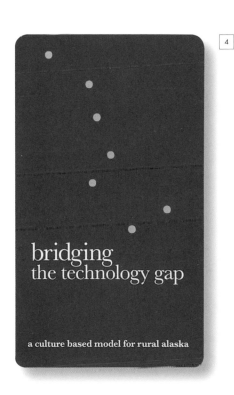

Steven C. Dinero Ph.D.
Associate Professor, Human Geography
School of General Studies

Philadelphia University
School House Lane & Henry Avenue
Philadelphia, PA 19144
tel. 215.951.2608 *fac.* 215.951.6888
e.mail dineros@philau.edu

bridging
the technology gap

a culture based model for rural alaska

1
design firm: SK+G Advertising
art director: Steve Averitt
designer: Steve Averitt
client: Avery Brooks +
        Associates Design
software/hardware: Adobe InDesign
paper/materials: Fox River Sundance Felt Warm
        White 100 lb cover, pearlescent
        foil and letterpressing

2
design firm: Louviere + Vanessa
art director: Jeff Louviere
designer: Jeff Louviere
client: Louviere + Vanessa
software/hardware: Adobe InDesign and Photoshop
paper/materials: 4 color offset

3
design firm: Sparc, Inc.
art director: Richard Cassis
designer: Richard Cassis
client: Yoga Laurie
software/hardware: Adobe Illustrator, InDesign,
        and Photoshop
paper/materials: Curious Collection Touch
        Soft Whipped Cream

4
design firm: Philadelphia University Design
art director: Frank Baseman
designer: Maria Ceara
client: Steven Dinero,
        Philadelphia University
software/hardware: Adobe Illustrator
paper/materials: Strathmore Cover,
        Offset printing with die-cuts

612 W. Main Street
Madison, WI 53703
SHINE ADVERTISING CO., LLC
P› 608 442 7373
F› 608 442 7374
WWW.SHINENORTH.COM

★

EMILIE SMITH
esmith@shinenorth.com

2

JENNA ADAMS
stylist

GENE SUELLENTROP

PRESIDENT

gene@inthesaucebrands.com

101 NORTH RIDGE ROAD
WICHITA, KANSAS 67212

PH 316-945-2277

FAX 316-945-2494

Gambino's Pizza · HERO DELI · AViVO BRICK OVEN PIZZERIA

WWW.INTHESAUCEBRANDS.COM

IN THE SAUCE BRANDS

TRADE MARK

www.scootcolumbus.com

scooter club

Cutters COLUMBUS

Cutters COLUMBUS

1

design firm: Shine Advertising
art director: Miek Kriefski
designer: Peter Bell
client: Shine Advertising

2

design firm: Interrobang Design
Collaborative
art director: Mark D. Sylvester
designer: Mark D. Sylvester
client: Jenna Adams, stylist
software/hardware: Adobe Illustrator CS2
paper/materials: Centura Gloss 100 lb cover
gloss laminate

3

design firm: Entermotion Design Studio
designer: Lea Morrow
client: Avivo Brick Oven Pizza and
In the Sauce Brands
software/hardware: Macromedia Freehand
paper/materials: Domtar Feltweave 3 color

4

design firm: Element
art director: Jeremy Slagle
client: Columbus Cutters
software/hardware: Adobe Photoshop, InDesign
and Illustrator

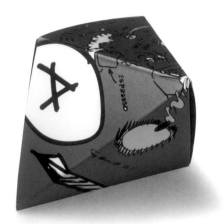

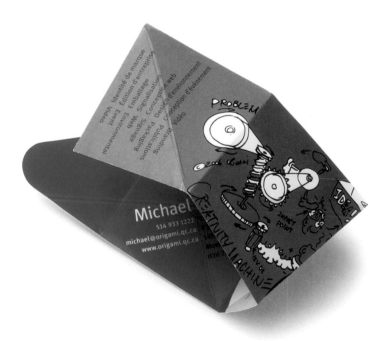

1	**2**	**3**
design firm: **Origami**	design firm: **Popcorn Initiative**	design firm: **BBM&D**
art director: **Michael Wou**	art director: **Chris Jones**	designer: **Barbara Brown**
illustrator: **Michael Wou**	designer: **Chris Jones**	client: **Jamal Edwards:**
client: **Origami**	client: **Popcorn Initiative**	**The Genius Organization**
software/hardware: **Adobe InDesign**	software/hardware: **Adobe Illustrator**	software/hardware: **Adobe Illustrator**

2

3

1

MELINDA FENTON

SAN FRANCISCO

MELINDA HENDERSON
PRESIDENT

P 415.567.8833 F 415.567.4216 E melinda@melindafenton.com

2

EMILY GONZALEZ

- *Project Coordinator* -

1060 N. CAPITOL AVENUE - SUITE E230
INDIANAPOLIS, INDIANA 46204

317.972.7870 P | F 317.972.7875
WWW.POLICYFIND.COM

CHEZ NOUS

A PLACE YOU DISCOVER.

PETER EVERETT IV
LE OWNER

ACEQUIA DE CORRALES
10700 CORRALES ROAD
CORRALES, NM 87114

PHONE | FAX
505.922.0333 | 505.922.0335

PEIV@DISCOVERCHEZNOUS.COM

DISCOVERCHEZNOUS.COM

3

4

B.L.A. Design Company

Brandi Lariscy Avant, designer

521 South Holly Street Columbia, SC 29205
Telephone: 803.518.4130 & 803.929.3233
e-mail: brandi@bladesignco.com

1

design firm: Helena Seo Design
art director: Helena Seo
designer: Helena Seo
client: Melinda Fenton
software/hardware: Adobe Illustrator

2

design firm: Timber Design Co.
art director: Lars Lawson
client: PolicyFind
software/hardware: Adobe Photoshop, Macromedia
Freehand, and Quark Xpress
paper/materials: Cougar Natural 100 lb cover

3

design firm: 3
art director: Sam Maclay
designer: Tim McGrath
client: Chez Nous
software/hardware: Quark Xpress and
Adobe Illustrator
paper/materials: Domtar Paper

4

design firm: B.L.A. Design Company
art director: Brandi Lariscy Avant
designer: Brandi Lariscy Avant
illustrator: Brandi Lariscy Avant
client: B.L.A. Design Company
software/hardware: Adobe Illustrator CS
paper/materials: 2 match colors, letterpress,
2-ply museum board

1

David Reinker, AIA
President
dreinker@sgpa.com

SGPA ARCHITECTURE AND PLANNING

SAN DIEGO · SAN FRANCISCO

1545 HOTEL CIRCLE SOUTH, STUDIO 200
SAN DIEGO, CALIFORNIA 92108

P. 619.297.0131 F. 619.294.9534 WWW.SGPA.COM

RETAIL
SENIOR LIVING
EDUCATION
MIXED-USE

2

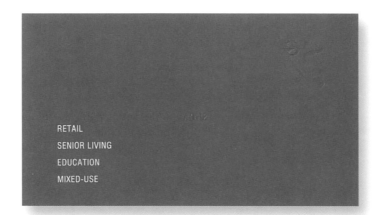

5151
santa fe street
suite h
san diego california
92109

SAN DIEGO
ORIGINAL

www.sanpasqualwinery.com

STEVE MAY *owner*

tel **619 846 4163**   fax **760 487 1065**
steve@sanpasqualwinery.com

Nicole Pierce
VICE PRESIDENT

68 Greenpoint Avenue, Suite 3
Brooklyn, NY 11222

(718) 349-2140 OFFICE
(718) 349-2972 FAX
(917) 723-2922 MOBILE

nicole@tyrannosaurusrecords.net
tyrannosaurusrecords.net

3

Joel G. Katz
Co-CEO

#7 Lakeway Centre
Suite 202
Austin, Texas 78735
Phone: 512.263.5730
Mobile: 512.751.4622
Fax: 512.263.5740
joel.katz@2mantour.com
www.2mantour.com

4

1

design firm: Blik
art director: Tyler Blik
designer: Yuki Hayashi
client: SGPA Architecture
software/hardware: Adobe CS
paper/materials: Beckett Enhance

2

design firm: Miriello Grafico
designer: Sallie Reynolds Allen
client: San Pasqual Winery
software/hardware: Adobe Illustrator

3

design firm: Alphabet Arm Design
art director: Aaron Belyea
designer: Ryan Frease
client: Tyrannosaurus Records
software/hardware: Adobe Illustrator

4

design firm: MBA
art director: Mark Brinkman and Mike Co
designer: Mark Brinkman
and Caroline Pledger
client: 2 Man Tour
software/hardware: Adobe Creative Suite
paper/materials: Neenah Classic Crest

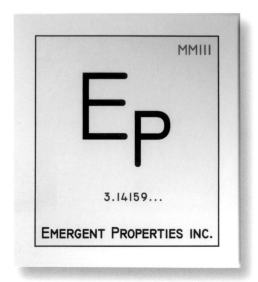

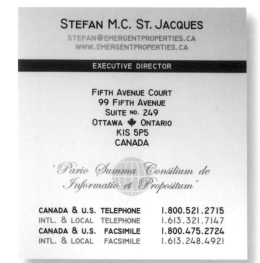

CHRISTY MERRINER

291 EAST 3RD STREET STUDIO 1B
NEW YORK, NEW YORK, 10009

TELEPHONE: 917-664-9940

CHRISTY@VINYL-CUT.COM

LOTTA ODELIUS ORD BILD FORM
www.lottaodelius.se mail@lottaodelius.se 0709-19 99 93

1

design firm: Emergent Properties
art director: Stefan M.C. St. Jacques
designer: Stefan M.C. St. Jacques
client: Emergent Properties

2

design firm: Limb Design
art director: Elise Desilva
designer: Emilie Desilva
client: Charmed Circle
software/hardware: Adobe InDesign
paper/materials: Paniere

3

design firm: Nothing: Something: NY
art director: Kevin Landwehr
designer: Kevin Landwehr
and Devin Becker
client: Vinyl-Cut Music Management
paper/materials: Bockingford
Triple-weight museum

4

design firm: Lotta Odelius Ord Bild Form
art director: Lotta Odelius
designer: Lotta Odelius
client: Lotta Odelius Ord Bild Form
software/hardware: Adobe Illustrator
paper/materials: Multi Design Original White
(papyrus), matte laminate and
spot-UV varnish (on one side).

1

2

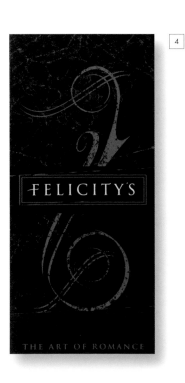

1

design firm: Miles Design
art director: Josh Miles
client: Simply She
software/hardware: Adobe Illustrator CS2
paper/materials: Cougar 100 lb White

2

design firm: Inovät
art director: Doug Logan
designer: Sean Hennessey
client: Inovät
software/hardware: Adobe Illustrator and Photoshop
paper/materials: Charcoal duplex and vellum

3

design firm: Willoughby Design Group
art director: Zack Shubkagel
and Ann Willoughby
(Creative director)
designer: Stephanie Lee
client: Feng

4

design firm: Greteman Group
art director: Sonia Greteman
designer: James Strange
client: Felicity's
(high-end lingerie, bath
and fragrance products)

1

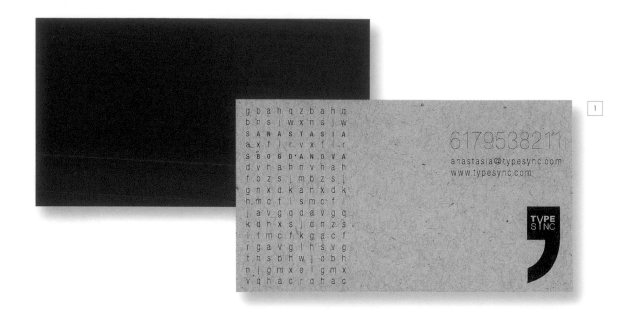

2

Kirk Smith

3400 South 2nd Street

Austin, TX 78704

512.699.4833

cyanmusiccollective.com

C Y A N

3

4

1

design firm: Typesync Studio
art director: Anastasia Bogdanova
designer: Anastasia Bogdanova
client: Typesync Studio
software/hardware: Adobe Illustrator CS2
paper/materials: Domtar

2

design firm: Entermotion Design Studios
designer: Lea Morrow
client: Small Town Treasures
software/hardware: Macromedia Freehand
paper/materials: Neenah Classic Columns,
3 Color

3

design firm: MBA
art director: Mark Brinkman
designer: Caroline Pledger
illustrator: Nick Butcher
client: Cyan
software/hardware: Adobe Creative Suite
paper/materials: Strathmore Ultimate White

4

design firm: Entermotion Design Studio
designer: Lea Morrow
client: Barbed Wire Trucking
software/hardware: Macromedia Freehand

Steve Arend President
543 W. Rich Street, Columbus, Ohio 43215
Tel 614.298.0430 Fax 614.298.0429 Cell 614.402.0344
sarend@arcconstruction.com

www.arcconconstruction.com

Jim Boggs Vice President
543 W. Rich Street, Columbus, Ohio 43215
Tel 614.298.0430 Fax 614.298.0429 Cell 614.402.0343
jboggs@arcconstruction.com

www.arcconconstruction.com

Steve Arend President
543 W. Rich Street, Columbus, Ohio 43215
Tel 614.298.0430 Fax 614.298.0429 Cell 614.402.0344
sarend@arcconstruction.com

www.arcconconstruction.com

Keith Scoby Superintendent
543 W. Rich Street, Columbus, Ohio 43215
Tel 614.298.0430 Fax 614.298.0429 Cell 614.419.4235

www.arcconconstruction.com

Unit 203, 30 Great Guildford St
London SE1 0HS

Phone/ 020 7633 0660
Fax/ 020 7401 9736
Email/ simon@kentlyons.com
www.kentlyons.com

Simon Hamilton

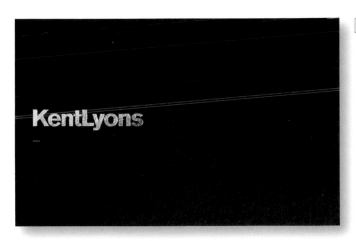

KentLyons

RENELL HUTTON *Controller*

THE DALLAS OPERA

CAMPBELL CENTRE I, 8350 NORTH CENTRAL EXPRESSWAY
SUITE 210, LB I-II, DALLAS, TEXAS 75206
Phone 214.443.1076 *Facsimile* 214.696.8978
RENELL@DALLASOPERA.ORG WWW.DALLASOPERA.ORG

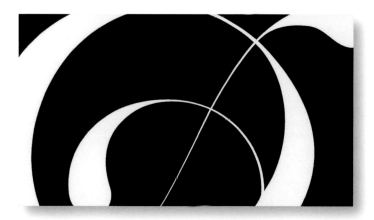

steam°

steam

steam

212 f

100 c

373 k

49 ontario street ste 500
toronto ontario m5a 2v1
telephone: 416.366.7050
facsimile: 416.366.7058
e:contact@steamfilms.ca

steam films inc.

1

CARLA VILHENA FITNESS CONSULTANT

carla@energyfxfitness.com
310.429.7476

ENERGY F/X™

13428 MAXELLA AVE #717, MARINA DEL REY, CA 90292

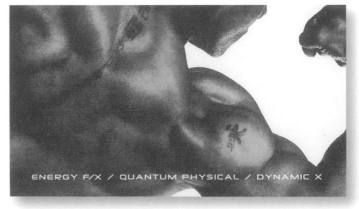

ENERGY F/X / QUANTUM PHYSICAL / DYNAMIC X

2

CHELSEA PARK
T O W N H O M E S

3

Dalana Morse
Sales Associate

Chelsea Park Sales Center
1206 Road to Six Flags • Arlington, Texas 76011
817.265.1000 *office* • 817.368.4020 *cell*
chelseaparklife.com • *dalana@chelseaparklife.com*

4

1

design firm: Blok
art director: Vanessa Eckstein
designer: Vanessa Eckstein
and Frances Chen
client: Steam
software/hardware: Adobe Illustrator
paper/materials: Strathmore Ultimate White

2

design firm: Evenson Design
art director: Stan Evenson
designer: Melanie Usas
client: Energy FX
software/hardware: EPS

3

design firm: Sibley Peteet Design—Dallas
art director: Don Sibley
designer: Brandon Kirk
client: Commercial Investment Services
software/hardware: Adobe Illustrator
paper/materials: Mohawk Superfine Ultra-white
Eggshell 130 double thick cover

4

design firm: Dottie Zimmerman,
Maryville University student
art director: (Professor) Laurie
Eisenbach-Bush
designer: Dottie Zimmerman,
Maryville University student
client: Dottie Zimmerman,
Maryville University student
software/hardware: Adobe Illustrator
paper/materials: Gilbert Clearfold 48 lb
printing: Epson Inkjet

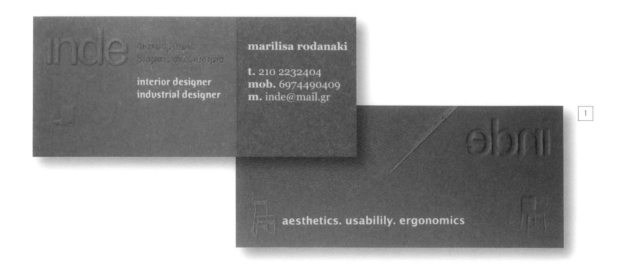

GAMBIT SOLUTIONS

info@gambitsolutions.com

610 Sixteenth Street #510   510 808 4107 /Tel
Oakland California 94612   510 808 4108 /Fax

business of IT

3

4

ΦΩΤΟΑΝΤΙΓΡΑΦΙΚΑ • ΑΝΑΛΩΣΙΜΑ • ΑΝΤΑΛΛΑΚΤΙΚΑ • SERVICE

ΝΙΚΟΣ ΚΥΡΙΑΚΟΠΟΥΛΟΣ

COPIELOR
Φρύνωνος 41 & Φιλολάου
Παγκράτι 116 32

Mob: 694 769 0 768
Tel: (+30) 210.75 24 0 64
Fax: (+30) 210.75 24 0 65
e-mail: info@copielor.com

www.copielor.com

copielor
office automation
merchandise & print

1

design firm: Di Depux
art director: Despina Bournele
designer: Despina Bournele
client: Marilisa Rodanaki
software/hardware: Adobe Illustrator CS
paper/materials: 2 Pantone, Zeta 250 gsm

2

design firm: Fangman Design
art director: Matt Fangman
designer: Matt Fangman
client: Blue Shoe Marketing
software/hardware: Adobe Illustrator
paper/materials: Classic Crest Solar White
100 lb cover

3

design firm: MINE™
art director: Christopher Simmons
designer: Christopher Simmons
and Tim Belonax
client: Gambit Solutions
software/hardware: Adobe Illustrator CS2
and InDesign CS2
paper/materials: Mohawk Superfine Ultrawhit
Smooth 130 lb DTC

4

design firm: Di Depux
art director: Despina Bournele
designer: Despina Bournele
client: Nikos Kyriakopoulos
software/hardware: Adobe Illustrator CS
paper/materials: 3 Pantone, Velvet finish

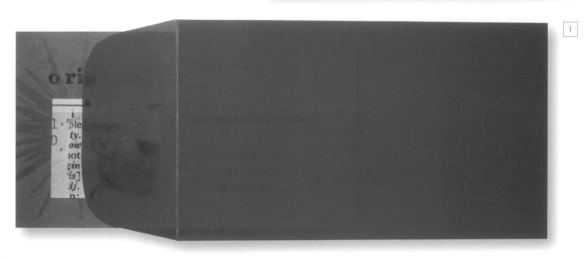

1

1

design firm: Originalia: A Design Studio
designer: Julie Mader-Meersman
illustrator: Julie Mader-Meersman
client: Originalia: A Design Studio
software/hardware: Adobe InDesign
paper/materials: Letterpress, French Durotone,
one-of-a-kind collage

2

design firm: Reactor
art director: Clifton Alexander
designer: Chase Wilson
client: Reactor
software/hardware: Adobe Illustrator
paper/materials: Esse Arancio, 100 lb cover

3

design firm: Blue Sky Design
art director: Tom Hart
designer: Tom Hart
illustrator: Tom Hart
client: Tom Hart
software/hardware: Royal Typewriter
paper/materials: Gmund's Bier Paper, self-made rubber
stamps, Archival "brilliance"
pigment inkpad

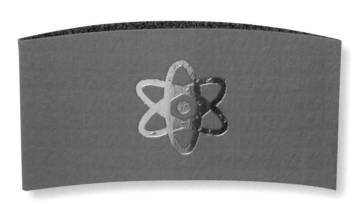

2

3

1

2

FSBDESIGN
FORMA&CONTEÚDO

WWW.FSBDESIGN.COM

11 3061 9596

FLÁVIO CARVALHO
DESIGNER

✉ flavio.carvalho@fsb.com.br
📱 11 8355 2249

r. pedroso alvarenga 900 7° andar
itaim bibi 04531 003
t. 11 3061.9596   f. 11 3086.0211

4

PURE ✕✕ SOURCE.™

IT starts here.

NAME : **HERBERT SAMUELS**
TITLE : President

ADDRESS : 437 East 51 Street   TELEPHONE : 347 365 2000
          Brooklyn, NY 11203   FACSIMILE : 360 365 2003
EMAIL : h.samuels@puresource.net
WEBSITE : **www.puresource.com**

1

design firm: Christiansen: Creative
designer: Tricia Christiansen
client: Christiansen: Creative
software/hardware: Quark Xpress
paper/materials: Fox River Sundance Felt

2

design firm: Miles Design
art director: Josh Miles
designer: Eric Folzenlogel
client: Purity Water Designs
software/hardware: Adobe Illustrator CS
paper/materials: 110 lb white cover/die

3

design firm: FSB Design
art director: Dora Medonça
and Flávio Carvalho
designer: Flávio Carvalho
client: FSB Design
software/hardware: Adobe Illustrator CS
paper/materials: dull couche, varnish stamp

4

design firm: 3rd Edge Communications
art director: Frankie Gonzalez
designer: Melissa Medina Mackin
client: Pure Source

AMY JO JURSICH, *designer*
3323 NORTH PAULINA NUMBER 2D
CHICAGO ILLINOIS 60657
T/F 773.525.9001 AJJURSICH@MSN.COM

1

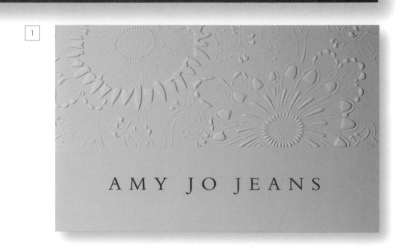

AMY JO JEANS

2

ANA RONCHA
DESIGNER

RUA CASSIANO BRANCO 43
4250-084 PORTO · PORTUGAL
T +351 933 428 805
E me@anaroncha.com
www.anaroncha.com

www.studiolello.com
7322 21st Avenue NW
Seattle Washington 98117
f: 206 297.7390

3

Bret Ashlee Watson
lello design + interiors
bretashlee@studiolello.com
m: 206 351.1599

lello

1		2		3	
design firm:	Pagliuco Design Company	design firm:	Ana Roncha	design firm:	Turnstyle
art director:	Michael Pagliuco	art director:	Ana Roncha	art director:	Ben Graham
designer:	Michael Pagliuco	designer:	Ana Roncha	designer:	Ben Graham
	and Amy Neiswander	client:	Ana Roncha	client:	Lello
client:	Amy Jo Jeans	software/hardware:	Freehand and Adobe Illustrator	software/hardware:	Adobe Illustrator

2

Mg
DESIGN

Mg

Meagan Goldberg
Graphic Designer

512 771 5430
www.meagangoldberg.com
meagan@meagangoldberg.com

3

Substância 4
comunicação e {design}

r. Almirante Tamandaré, 66 - sl. 1215 • Flamengo • RJ
cep 22210-060 { t.: 55 21 2205 4959 / 3507 3452}
substancia4@substancia4.com.br • www.substancia4.com.br

1

design firm:	Willoughby Design Group
art director:	Nicole Satterwhite and
	(Creative directors)
	Ann Willoughby and
	Megan Semrick
designer:	Stephanie Lee and
	Jessica McEntire

2

design firm:	Meagan Goldberg
art director:	Meagan Goldberg
designer:	Meagan Goldberg
client:	Meagan Goldberg
software/hardware:	Adobe Illustrator CS, MAC

3

design firm:	Substância 4 Comunicação e Design
art director:	Carolina Terra and
	Marcia Albuquerque
designer:	Marcia Albuquerque and
	Carolina Terra
client:	Substância 4 Comunicação e Design
software/hardware:	Corel Draw 10

1

Suzanne Holzworth
P R I N T M A K E R

suzanne@worthitstudio.com
www.worthitstudio.com

Suzanne Holzworth
P R I N T M A K E R

suzanne@worthitstudio.com
www.worthitstudio.com

Suzanne Holzworth
P R I N T M A K E R

suzanne@worthitstudio.com
www.worthitstudio.com

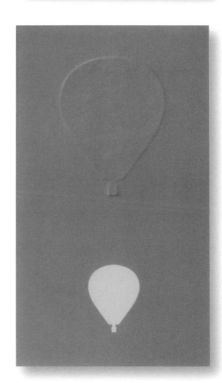

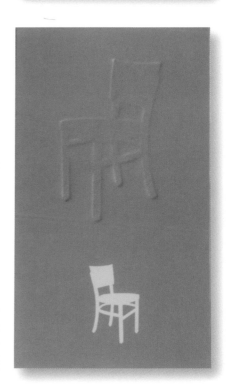

Bill Henderly, CFA
Nvest Wealth Strategies, Inc.

2310 Home Road
Delaware, Ohio 43015
740.917.9234
bill@nvestwealth.com

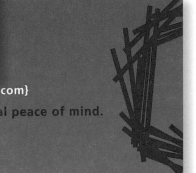

2

{www.nvestwealth.com}
Delivering financial peace of mind.

WENDY WRAY
CHIEF OPERATING OFFICER

T 604 921 1321
E wendy@wraygroup.com

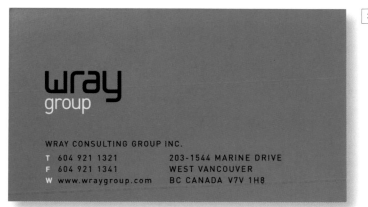

3

WRAY CONSULTING GROUP INC.
T 604 921 1321   203-1544 MARINE DRIVE
F 604 921 1341   WEST VANCOUVER
W www.wraygroup.com   BC CANADA V7V 1H8

jungeschachtel

chachtel.de

kleiner aufma

1

design firm: Jungeschachtel

art director: Nina Dautzenberg and
Andrea Gadesmann

client: Jungeschachtel

software/hardware: Adobe Illustrator

paper/materials: Distinction

1

2

NOMAD LOUNGE

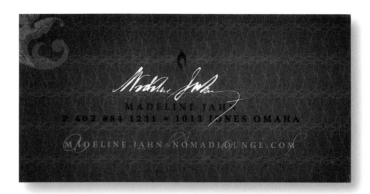

MADELINE JAHN
P 402 884 1231 • 1013 JONES OMAHA

MADELINE.JAHN@NOMADLOUNGE.COM

4

SIENNA
EST 1987
GRAPHICS INC

MARTIN ZENOR
PRESIDENT

ADDRESS	PHONE/FAX	EMAIL
5701 NE 19TH TERRACE	P 954.612.2730	SIENNAG@
FT LAUDERDALE, FL 33308	F 954.776.1155	BELLSOUTH.NET

Andy Fetsch
General Manager

Phone: 651.216.2472
Fax: 651.257.5624

25884 Quail Ridge Trail
Lindstrom, MN 55045

andy@gofetsch.com
www.gofetsch.com

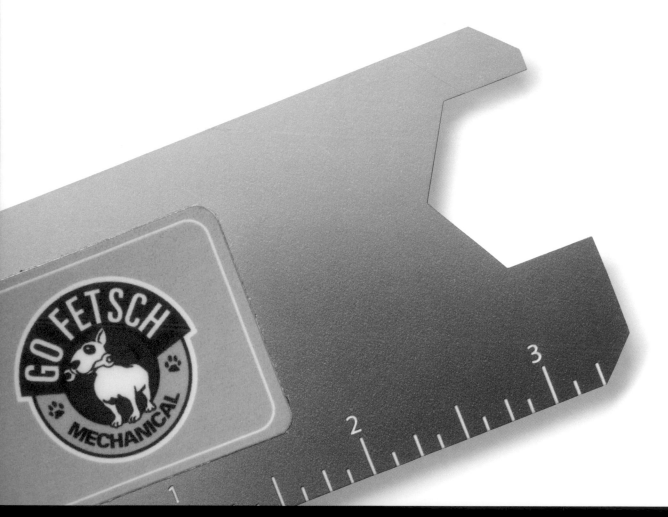

	1		2		3
design firm:	Red Circle Agency	design firm:	MINE™	design firm:	smashLAB
art director:	Matt Benka	art director:	Christopher Simmons	art director:	Eric Karjaluoto
designer:	Bryan Dunn	designer:	Christopher Simmons	designer:	Robert Young
client:	Go Fetsch Mechanical	client:	Steel Media	client:	NUGSS
software/hardware:	Adobe Illustrator	software/hardware:	Adobe Illustrator and InDesign CS2	software/hardware:	Adobe Illustrator
paper/materials:	Stainless steel, vinyl laminate	paper/materials:	Mohawk Superfine Ultrawhite smooth DTC 160 lb and brightwhite uncoated permanent label GPA 60 lb	paper/materials:	Topkote dull-coated

RICHARD STEEL
President

NY/ 917 405 8590
LA/ 310 346 3455

rich@steelmediainc.com

STEEL MEDIA

49 West 69th Street Suite 2A
New York NY 10023
www.steelmediainc.com

Simone Renaud
Ombudsperson

nugss UNBC Northern Undergraduate Student Society
3333 University Way, Prince George, BC, V2N 4Z9

T. 250.960.6427   F. 250.960.5617
E. ombuds@nugss.com
www.nugss.com

1

MEMO

8912 Spanish Ridge Avenue
Las Vegas, Nevada 89148
T 702 478 4000 F 702 478 4001

SK+G

Stephen Averitt
Executive Design Director

T 702 478 4000   F 702 478 4001
steve.averitt@skgadv.com
8912 Spanish Ridge Avenue
Las Vegas, Nevada 89148

SK+G
skgadv.com

8912 Spanish Ridge Avenue
Las Vegas, Nevada 89148

8912 Spanish Ridge Avenue
Las Vegas, Nevada 89148

2

reality digital

Cynthia Francis / CEO

600 Townsend St, Ste 170e, San Francisco, CA 94103
415.503.3959 o / 415.760.4717 m / 415.437.2892 f
www.realitydigital.com / cfrancis@realitydigital.com

travelbeam
leisure travel

Eileen Allan

10 The Downs Altrincham Cheshire United Kingdom WA14 2PU
Telephone +44(0)161 928 6777 Fax +44(0)161 928 6333
Email eileen.allan@travelbeam.co.uk Web www.travelbeam.co.uk

3

We speak
the language
of your lab

4

PRŌMIUM
The environmental LIMS company

Bobby Sims
Technical Support Specialist

bsims@promium.com

359 Banning Street, Suite B
Marshfield, MO 65706

PH 425.286.9200 EXT 265
FX 425.286.9201

promium.com

1

design firm: SK+G Advertising
art director: Steve Averitt
designer: Ralwa Lee
client: SK+G Advertising
software/hardware: Adobe Illustrator and InDesign
paper/materials: Mohawk Navajo

2

design firm: Helena Seo Design
art director: Helena Seo
designer: Helena Seo
client: Reality Digital
software/hardware: Adobe Illustrator
paper/materials: Starwhite Sirius Smooth
130 lb DTC

3

design firm: Imagine
art director: David Caunce
designer: David Caunce
client: Travelbeam
software/hardware: Adobe Illustrator
paper/materials: Conqueror CX22

4

design firm: Belyea
art director: Ron Lars Hansen
designer: Ron Lars Hansen
client: Promium
software/hardware: Adobe Illustrator and InDesign
paper/materials: Neenah Environment

INSTITUT DU LASER CUTANÉ DE L'OUTAOUAIS
200, rue Montcalm, bureau 302, Gatineau (Québec) J8Y 3B5

ULTRa_DESIGN

braulio lacerda carollo
braulio@ultradesign.com.br

rua padre anchieta 2454
conjunto 503
curitiba 80730 000

www.ultradesign.com.br
ultra@ultradesign.com.br

41 3016 3023

DESIGNYƎ⅃MƎ⅃

$19.86

1 20628 56900 7

Lemley Design is a leader in branded customer experience at retail.

LEMLEY DESIGN CAN BE BLEACHED IF NEEDED, DRY FLAT

DESIꓱⅬMƎ⅃

DIANA FRYC Director of Business Development

ADDRESS 2727 FAIRVIEW AVE. E, SUITE F, SEATTLE, WA 98102, USA

TELEPHONE **206 285 6900** x202 / FACSIMILE 206 285 6906

INTERNET www.lemleydesign.com / EMAIL diana@lemleydesign.com

SELTZER
design inteLLigence

4

ROCHELLE SELTZER, AIGA ○ president

SELTZER 45 Newbury Street, Suite 406 | Boston MA 02116
617 353 0303 *t* | 617 262 0255 *f* | seltzerdesign.com | rs@seltzerdesign.com

1
design firm: Kolegram
art director: Gontran Blais
designer: Gontran Blais
client: ILCO (Institut du Laser Cutané
la de L'outaouais)
paper/materials: Domtar Solutions

2
design firm: Ultra Design
art director: Braulio Carollo
designer: Braulio Carollo
client: Ultra Design
software/hardware: Adobe Illustrator
paper/materials: Couche Matte

3
design firm: Lemley Design
art director: David Lemley
designer: Kim Toda
client: Lemley Design
paper/materials: Mohawk Superfine

4
design firm: Seltzer
art director: Rochelle Seltzer
designer: Meaghan O'Keefe
client: Seltzer
software/hardware: Adobe InDesign
paper/materials: Strathmore 25% Cotton,
Soft white, 100 lb woven cover

1

1

design firm: Bennett Holzworth Design
art director: Bennett Holzworth
client: Be a Design Group
software/hardware: Adobe Illustrator, InDesign,
and Photoshop
paper/materials: Letterpress, stickers,
photopolymer plates,
Neenah Eames

A GRAPHIC DESIGN BLOG

BE A DESIGN GROUP

Adrian Hanft
adrian@beadesigngroup.com
www.beadesigngroup.com

A GRAPHIC DESIGN BLOG

BE A DESIGN GROUP

Bennett Holzworth
bennett@beadesigngroup.com
www.beadesigngroup.com

A GRAPHIC DESIGN BLOG

BE A DESIGN GR

Bennett Holzwort
tt@beadesigngrou

Scott VanKirk
ARTISTIC DIRECTOR

SVANKIRK@EXPODESIGN.NET
T: 317.784.5610
M: 317.523.5583
F: 317.784.5724

5906 SOUTH HARDING ST INDIANAPOLIS, IN 46205

Jay Parnell
317.366.1680
gomezblack@jayparnell.com
www.jayparnell.com

1

design firm: Ana Roncha
art director: Ana Roncha
designer: Ana Roncha
client: DEED
software/hardware: Macromedia Freehand
and Adobe Illustrator CS
paper/materials: Couché Date with
varnish on one side

2

design firm: Switch Creative
art director: Michael Carpenter
designer: Michael Carpenter
client: SteVan Lazich
software/hardware: Adobe Illustrator
paper/materials: Silk cards and foil

3

design firm: Miles Design
art director: Josh Miles
designer: Eric Folzenlogel
client: Harmony X:
United Artists of Expodesign
software/hardware: Adobe Illustrator CS2
paper/materials: French Cement 100 lb

4

design firm: Miles Design
art director: Josh Miles
designer: Eric Folzenlogel
client: Jay Parnell
software/hardware: Adobe Illustrator CS2
paper/materials: French Kraft 100 lb,
thermo die-cut

ANA PAULA RODRIGUES
DIRECTORA ADMINISTRATIVA

RUA FERNÃO VAZ DOURADO 62
4150-322 PORTO PORTUGAL
T +351 226 165 569
F +351 226 165 570
E ana.paula@ska.pt
www.ska.pt

JORGE JORGE
HEAD OF DESIGN

RUA FERNÃO VAZ DOURADO 62
4150-322 PORTO PORTUGAL
T +351 226 165 571
F +351 226 165 570
M +351 969 508 795
E jorge.jorge@ska.pt
www.ska.pt

LUIS MAGNO
DIRECTOR DE PRODUÇÃO

RUA FERNÃO VAZ DOURADO 62
4150-322 PORTO PORTUGAL
T +351 226 165 563
F +351 226 165 570
M +351 969 508 793
E luis.magno@ska.pt
www.ska.pt

1

hi-five!

bernstein-rein
4600 madison avenue
kansas city, missouri 64112
bernsteinrein.com

franklin m. oviedo **design creative**
frankoviedo@bradv.com

816 960 5485 direct
816 399 6485 fax
816 756 0640 agency

2

LyndonWade
lyndon.wade@rushwade2.com *t* 816 421 0011 *c* 816 529 9971
2010 McGee Kansas City, Missouri 64108 • lyndonwade.com

rushwade2
PHOTOGRAPHY + DIGITAL IMAGING

3

1

design firm: SKA
art director: Jorge Jorge
designer: Jorge Jorge
client: SKA
software/hardware: Freehand
paper/materials: Couche Date and Verniz

2

design firm: BR
art director: Franklin Oviedo, Anthony Magliano,
Krista Masilionis, and Chuck Hoffman
designer: Franklin Oviedo and Anthony Magliano
writer: Brent Anderson
client: Bernstein-Rein Advertising
software/hardware: Adobe Illustrator and Photoshop
paper/materials: Classic Crest Natural

3

design firm: BR
art director: Franklin Oviedo, Anthony Magliano,
Krista Masilionis, and Chuck Hoffman
designer: Franklin Oviedo and Anthony Magliano
writer: Brent Anderson
client: Rush Wade 2 Photography
software/hardware: Adobe Illustrator and Photoshop
paper/materials: Classic Crest Natural

3

cheryl dailey
tel 408.219.8866
email cheryl@dailey.info
web cheryl.dailey.info
san francisco bay area

CHERYL DAILEY
MAKEUP+HAIR

4

measure twice
YOU ONLY BUILD ONCE.

www.measure2.com

NAME:
Jeff King / General Contractor

ADDRESS:
P.O. Box 10393, Bozeman, MT 59719

PHONE: EMAIL:
406.581.2246   jeff@measure2.com

measure twice
YOU ONLY BUILD ONCE.

GENERAL CONTRACTOR / CUSTOM HOME CONSTRUCTION / REMODELS

1

design firm: Zande + Newman Design
art director: Adam Newman
designer: Jan Bertman and Loren Stephens
client: Kenneth's Studio for Hair
software/hardware: Adobe InDesign
paper/materials: Mohawk Superfine

2

design firm: David Clark Design
art director: David Clark
designer: Becky Gelder
client: David Clark Design
software/hardware: Adobe Illustrator CS
paper/materials: Classic Crest Solar White
80 lb cover, Fasson
printing: Western Printing

3

design firm: AngryPorcupine*Design
art director: Cheryl Roder-Quill
designer: Cheryl Roder-Quill
client: Cheryl Dailey Makeup and Hair
software/hardware: Adobe Illustrator
paper/materials: Curious Metallics;
1 PMS and black
printing: Carr Printing Company
(Bountiful, UT)

4

design firm: 3
art director: Sam Maclay
designer: Tim McGrath
illustrator: Tim McGrath
client: Measure Twice
software/hardware: Quark Xpress and
Adobe Illustrator
paper/materials: French Paper
and printed labels

1

2

KEVIN AKERS

design + imagery

P 925-735-1015
F 925-735-1014

4095 LILAC RIDGE RD
SAN RAMON, CA 94583

www.kevinakers.com

1

RIVER BLUFF

[architects]

RONALD D. FUSTON, AIA

[1214 FREDERICK AVE | ST JOSEPH MO 64501]

TEL 816 232 7248 | FAX 816 233 3319
E-MAIL RFUSTON@RIVERBLUFF.COM

2

3

ISABELLE MEUNIER
ASSISTANT VINICULTEUR
ASSISTANT VINEYARD MANAGER & WINEMAKER

T 905 562 9404
F 905 562 9407
E isabelle.meunier@leclosjordanne.com
W leclosjordanne.com

2540 South Service Road
Jordan Station, ON, Canada L0R 1S0

alex coletti
ph: 212 654 5091
fx: 212 654 9287
alex.coletti@mtvstaff.com

770 Broadway
New York NY 10003

alex coletti
productions

4

1

design firm: Kevin Akers Design and Imagery
art director: Kevin Akers
designer: Kevin Akers
illustrator: Kevin Akers
client: Kevin Akers
software/hardware: Adobe Illustrator
paper/materials: letterpress

2

design firm: Design Ranch
art director: Michelle Sonderegger
and Ingred Sidie
designer: Michelle Sonderegger
and Ingred Sidie
client: River Bluff
software/hardware: Adobe Illustrator

3

design firm: Dossier Creative, Inc.
art director: Don Chisholm
designer: Patrick Smith
client: Vincor International
software/hardware: Adobe Illustrator and InDesign
paper/materials: Laminated paper
Front: Tomahawk, cool white
80 lb cover;
Back: Topkote 78 lb dull cover

4

design firm: Think Studio, NYC
art director: John Clifford
designer: John Clifford
illustrator: John Clifford
client: Alex Coletti Productions
software/hardware: Adobe Photoshop and
Illustrator, Quark Xpress
paper/materials: Mohawk Superfine

1

2

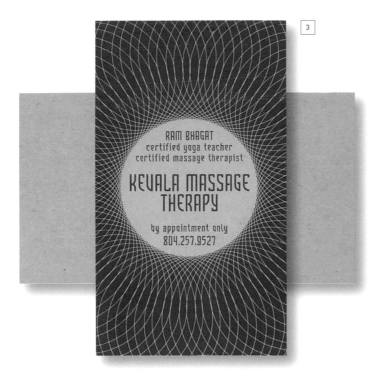

RAM BHAGAT
certified yoga teacher
certified massage therapist

KEVALA MASSAGE
THERAPY

by appointment only
804.257.9527

3

lieto
GIFTS OF
GRATITUDE

Danyel Mele

ring 503.705.8633   danyel@lieto-pdx.com   lieto-pdx.com

4

1
design firm: Ace Architects
art director: Adam Gillett
designer: Adam Gillett
client: Ace Architects
software/hardware: Photoshop
paper/materials: Coated

2
design firm: Funnel: Eric Kass: Utilitarian +
Commercial + Fine: Art
art director: Eric Kass
designer: Eric Kass
client: Funnel
software/hardware: Adobe Illustrator CC
paper/materials: Process Offset on Coated White
cover with film laminate

3
design firm: Another Limited Rebellion
art director: Noah Scalin
designer: Noah Scalin
client: Ram Bhagat–
Kevala Massage Therapy
software/hardware: Adobe Illustrator
paper/materials: Genesis Marigold

4
design firm: Dotzero Design
designer: Karen Wippich and Jon Wippich
client: Lieto
software/hardware: Adobe Illustrator and Photoshop
paper/materials: Cougar 80 lb cover

1

Jim Van Kerkhove

Prolifiq Software
4145 SW Watson Ave.
Suite 450
Beaverton, OR 97005

E   jimv@prolifiq.net
O   +1 503 684 1415
M   +1 503 539 1415
W   www.prolifiq.net

PROLIFIQ

2

WENDY OWEN
PRINCIPAL

300 BRANNAN STREET NO.406
SAN FRANCISCO CALIFORNIA 94107
T 415 227 4235 F 415 227 4261
WENDY@GIANTANT.COM

GIANT**ANT**

3

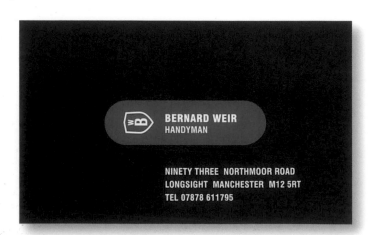

BERNARD WEIR
HANDYMAN

NINETY THREE NORTHMOOR ROAD
LONGSIGHT MANCHESTER M12 5RT
TEL 07878 611795

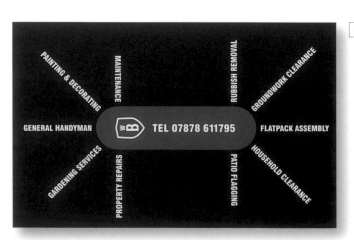

PAINTING & DECORATING
MAINTENANCE
RUBBISH REMOVAL
GROUNDWORK CLEARANCE
GENERAL HANDYMAN   TEL 07878 611795   FLATPACK ASSEMBLY
GARDENING SERVICES
PROPERTY REPAIRS
PATIO FLAGGING
HOUSEHOLD CLEARANCE

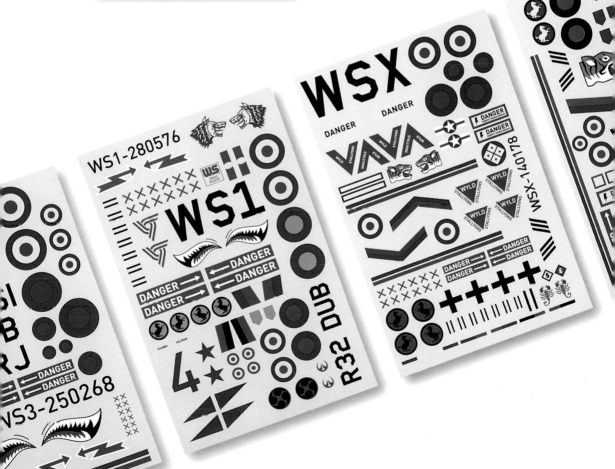

1

kelly ring   kelly@awakeningorganics.com

2535 w night owl phoenix, az 85085

tel 623 271 9426 fax 623 271 9427 **cell 623 229 6655**

1

design firm: Firebelly Design

art director: Dawn Hancock

2

design firm: Turnstyle

art director: Ben Graham

3

design firm: EPOS, Inc.

art director: Gabrielle Raumberger

2

turquoise

oise

oise

misha zadeh
misha@turquoisecreative.com

fine stationery + design
7031 12th avenue nw
seattle washington 98117
fax 206.783.0572
phone 206.783.5993

misha zadeh
@turquoisecreative.com

fine stationery + design
7031 12th avenue nw
seattle washington 98117
fax 206.783.0572
phone 206.783.5993

misha zadeh
@turquoisecreative.com

fine stationery + design
7031 12th avenue nw
seattle washington 98117
fax 206.783.0572
phone 206.783.5993

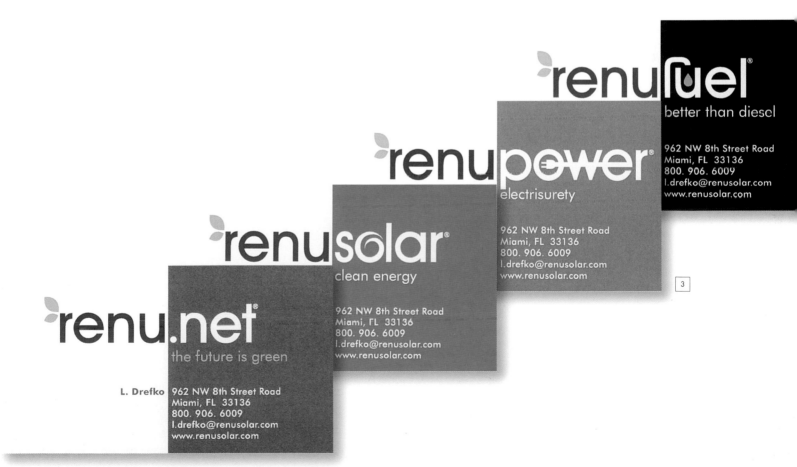

renufuel®
better than diesel

962 NW 8th Street Road
Miami, FL 33136
800. 906. 6009
l.drefko@renusolar.com
www.renusolar.com

renupower®
electrisurety

962 NW 8th Street Road
Miami, FL 33136
800. 906. 6009
l.drefko@renusolar.com
www.renusolar.com

renusolar®
clean energy

962 NW 8th Street Road
Miami, FL 33136
800. 906. 6009
l.drefko@renusolar.com
www.renusolar.com

renu.net®
the future is green

L. Drefko 962 NW 8th Street Road
Miami, FL 33136
800. 906. 6009
l.drefko@renusolar.com
www.renusolar.com

3

1

Suzanne Boccalatte Design Director

Telephone 61 2 9310 4309 I Mobile 0412 050 090
PO Box 370 Surry Hills NSW 2010 Sydney Australia
Studio 43. 61 Marlborough St Surry Hills NSW 2010
suzanne@boccalatte.com I boccalatte.com

2

3

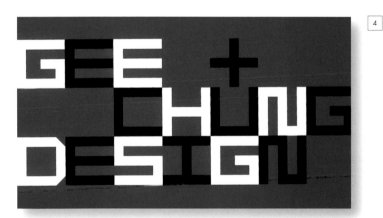

4

1

design firm: Boccalatte
art director: Suzanne Boccalatte
designer: Suzanne Boccalatte
client: Boccalatte
software/hardware: Adobe Illustrator
and InDesign CS
paper/materials: Knight Smooth Cream,
Verco type 350 gsm

2

design firm: Color Cubic
art director: Michael John and Christy Lai
designer: Christy Lai
client: Color Cubic
software/hardware: Adobe Illustrator and InDesign
paper/materials: Silk Laminate

3

design firm: Subplot Design, Inc.
art director: Matthew Clark and Roy White
designer: Matthew Clark
client: Change Advertising
software/hardware: Adobe Illustrator
paper/materials: Mohawk Options

4

design firm: Gee + Chung Design
art director: Earl Gee
designer: Earl Gee
client: Gee + Chung Design
software/hardware: Adobe Illustrator and InDesign
paper/materials: Mohawk Superfine 130 lb cover

1

2

ΚΑΤΕΡΙΝΑ ΒΕΝΙΟΥ
ΔΙΑΚΟΣΜΗΤΡΙΑ

mob. **6944.91.99.48**

1

design firm: Di Depux
art director: Despina Bournele
designer: Despina Bournele
client: Ioannis Ragavas
software/hardware: Adobe Illustrator CS
paper/materials: CMYK, Velvet 350 grade

2

design firm: Di Depux
art director: Despina Bournele
designer: Despina Bournele
client: Di Depux
software/hardware: Adobe Illustrator CS
paper/materials: 2 Pantone, Curious Met
A067, 250 grade

3

design firm: Di Depux
art director: Despina Bournele
designer: Despina Bournele
client: Katerina Veniou,
Eleni Akermanoglou
software/hardware: Adobe Illustrator CS
paper/materials: CMYK, Velvet 350 grade

4

design firm: Di Depux
art director: Despina Bournele
designer: Despina Bournele
client: Dora
software/hardware: Adobe Illustrator CS
paper/materials: CMYK, Velvet 350 grade

TROY VERRETT, CSI, CDT
principal
tv@insitedevelopments.com
504.610.7238 CELL

Insite Developments, LLC
Building 11935, Suite 3
N.E. Nineteenth Drive
North Miami FL 33181
954.854.4312 TEL
504.412.9796 FAX

WWW.INSITEDEVELOPMENTS.COM

architectural services
real estate development
planning

architectural services
real estate development
planning

WWW.INSITEDEVELOPMENTS.COM

NEW ORLEANS | MIAMI

TROY VERRETT, CSI, CDT
principal
tv@insitedevelopments.com
504.610.7238 CELL

Insite Developments, LLC
822 Perdido Street
Suite 101
New Orleans LA 70112
504.412.9797 TEL
504.412.9796 FAX

in|site

1

ANGARA

ANKUR DAGA
CHIEF EXECUTIVE OFFICER

15 WEST 47TH STREET, SUITE 1303, NEW YORK, NY 10036
TEL. 877 9 ANGARA FAX. 201 503 8159 WWW.ANGARA.COM
CELL. 646 705 3999 ANKUR.DAGA@ANGARA.COM

2

panecaldo

ANTHONY CEDICCI

pane caldo ~ contemporary italian cuisine
72 East Walton Street CHICAGO 60611
312 649 0055 *f* 274 0540
anthony@pane-caldo.com

3

4

Lolight

Aaron Deckler
7106 A Woodhue Ct.
Austin TX 78745
T:512.587.7590
F:866.494.8194
aaron@lolight.com
www.lolight.com

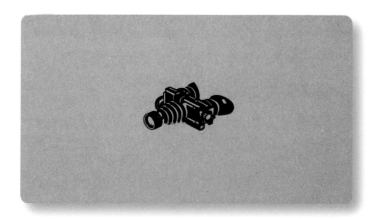

1

design firm: Zande + Newman Design
art director: Adam Newman
designer: Adam Newman
client: In Site Developments
software/hardware: Adobe Illustrator
paper/materials: Mohawk Superfine

2

design firm: Helena Seo Design
art director: Helena Seo
designer: Helena Seo
client: Angara, Inc.
software/hardware: Adobe Illustrator

3

design firm: Pagliuco Design Company
art director: Michael Pagliuco
designer: Michael Pagliuco
client: Pane Caldo
paper/materials: Strathmore

4

design firm: Lolight Design
art director: Aaron Deckler
designer: Aaron Deckler
client: Lolight Design
software/hardware: Adobe Illustrator and InDesign
paper/materials: Gilbert Esse White Green
printing: Offset printing 2/2

Lisa Evano
Account Supervisor   counterpartCD.com

lisa@
counterpartCD.com   901   323-4900 T
578-7878 F

40 South Idlewild Memphis TN 38104

THE VOICE OF THE BRAND

THE EAR OF THE CUSTOMER

communication +
COUNTERPART design

2

PNL Pour se comprendre

PNL

Paul Mercier
Conseiller / enseignant

Centre de formation en Programmation Neuro Linguistique
C.P. 79158 / Gatineau (Qc) / J8Y 6V2 / centreformationpnl.com
t 819 770-5117 / f 819 777-6333 pmercier@centreformationpnl.com

3

Leslie
Cakora
Netzky
Archivist.
Designer.

Leslie
Cakora
Netzky
Archivist.
Designer.
Stylist.
Jeweler.
Cultural
Anthropologist.
Creative
Force.

655 Deerfield Road
Suite 100, No. 324
Deerfield, Illinois 60015

T 312 282 7515
F 646 219 0443
leslie@cakora.com

www.cakora.com

1

design firm: Counterpart Communication Design
art director: Sheperd Simmons
designer: David Fuller and Mike Powell
client: Counterpart Communication Design
with Product Artist Anna Hatton
software/hardware: Adobe Illustrator and Quark Xpress
paper/materials: Beckett Enhance, Arctic, 80 lb cover

2

design firm: Kolegram
art director: Jean-Luc Denat
designer: Martin Poirier
client: Centre de Formation
en Programmation
Neuro-Linguistique

3

design firm: Liska + Associates
art director: Steve Liska
designer: Vanessa Oltmanns
client: Leslie Cakora Netzky
software/hardware: Adobe Illustrator and InDesign
paper/materials: Sleeve: Classic Crest 80 lb cover;
Card: Classic Crest 100 lb cover

948 SOUTH COOPER
MEMPHIS TN 38104
ph: 901.276.0002
dishmemphis.com

dish dish dish

CHRIS GARCIA
ph: 901.497.0463
chris@dishmemphis.com

BAR MANAGER   DEEJAY   GENERAL MANAGER

1

HONEY inspired american dining

42 Shewell Avenue   Doylestown, Pennsylvania 18901

Joe & Amy McAtee, Proprietors   CELL 215.230.9936

h BUCKS COUNTY HONEY

2

CHRIS ROONEY

illustration ✳ design

TELEPHONE 415.TCR.DRAW
LOONEYROONEY@MINDSPRING.COM
WWW.LOONEYROONEY.COM

3

CHRIS ROONEY

illustration ✳ design

TELEPHONE 415.TCR.DRAW
LOONEYROONEY@MINDSPRING.COM
WWW.LOONEYROONEY.COM

HOT SAKĒ

4

JASON HAUSMAN
Creative
704/906/3136 / jason@hotsakecreative.com
www.hotsakecreative.com_1510 Camden Road / Charlotte_NC 28203
A CREATIVE ARTS COMPANY

1

design firm: Switch Creative
art director: Michael Carpenter
designer: Michael Carpenter
client: SmartCity
software/hardware: Adobe Illustrator
paper/materials: Silk finish

2

design firm: Johnston Duffy
art director: Martin Duffy
designer: Andy Evans and Martin Duffy
client: Honey Restaurant
software/hardware: Adobe Illustrator
and Photoshop on MAC
paper/materials: Mohawk Superfine

3

design firm: Chris Rooney Illustration/Design
designer: Chris Rooney
illustrator: Chris Rooney
client: Chris Rooney
software/hardware: Adobe Illustrator
paper/materials: 15 pt Tango C1S

4

design firm: A3 Design
art director: Amanda Altman
designer: Alan Altman
client: Hot Saké
software/hardware: Adobe Illustrator

THIELEN DESIGNS
115 GOLD AVE. SUITE 209
*ALBUQUERQUE, NM
87104
SALE
.02¢
505 205 3157
WWW.THIELENDESIGNS.COM
~~49.95 USD~~

Tony Thielen
Tony@ThielenDesigns.com

XL

3

4

LIVESTRONG™
LANCE ARMSTRONG FOUNDATION

PO BOX 161150
AUSTIN, TX 78716-1150

TEL 512.236.8820
FAX 512.236.8482

INSPIRING AND EMPOWERING
PEOPLE AFFECTED BY CANCER

LIVESTRONG.ORG

UNITY IS STRENGTH. KNOWLEDGE IS POWER. ATTITUDE IS EVERYTHING.

ASSISTANCE FOR CANCER SURVIVORS: 866.235.7205

1

design firm: Element
art director: John McCollum
designer: Jeremy Slagle
client: Element
software/hardware: Adobe Illustrator and InDesign

2

design firm: Hartford Design
art director: Tim Hartford
designer: Scott Hight
client: Great Kitchens
software/hardware: Adobe Illustrator
and InDesign CS

3

design firm: Thielen Designs
art director: Tony Thielen
designer: Tony Thielen
client: Thielen Designs
software/hardware: Adobe Illustrator
paper/materials: Classic Crest Natural 103 DTC,
letterpress, Cougar 80 lb cover,
eyelets, XL clothing stickers,
price tags

4

design firm: Lance Armstrong Foundation
in-house design
art director: Diana Guentzel
designer: Diana Guentzel
client: Lance Armstrong Foundation
software/hardware: Adobe Illustrator and
Photoshop, and Quark Xpress
paper/materials: Classic Crest Solar White
Smooth 110 lb cover

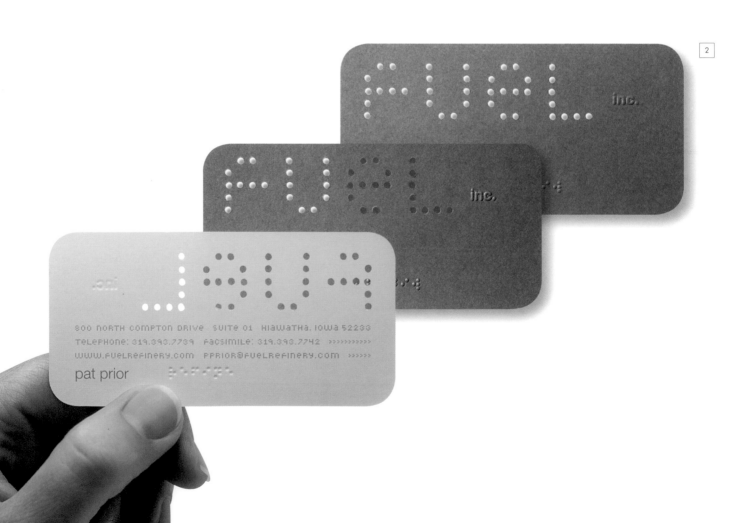

3

3 THINGS YOU SHOULD
KNOW ABOUT MELISSA:

She has castrated a goat.
She is fluent in Pig Latin.
She kind of likes beets.

MELISSA GEORGE
Production Manager

8220 LA MIRADA, SUITE 500
ALBUQUERQUE, NM 87109
email: mgeorge@whois3.com
phone: 505.293.2333
fax: 505.293.1198

STRATEGY / ADVERTISING / DESIGN

4

MIKE EATON
Senior Art Director

13 Water Street, Holliston, MA 01746
v 508-429-0755 x18
f 508-429-0766
w www.m-d-g.com
e meaton@m-d-g.com

MDG INC

1

design firm: LeBoYe
art director: Ignatius Hermawan Tanzil
designer: Ignatius Hermawan Tanzil
and Ismiaji Cahyono
client: LeBoYe
software/hardware: Freehand MX
paper/materials: Curious 120 gsm and
Conqueror Wove 250 gsm

2

design firm: Fuel
designer: Bill Bollman and Brian Cox
client: Fuel
software/hardware: Adobe Illustrator
paper/materials: Mohawk Superfine

3

design firm: 3
art director: Sam Maclay
designer: Tim McGrath
illustrator: Tim McGrath
client: 3
software/hardware: Quark Xpress and
Adobe Illustrator
paper/materials: French Paper, gummed labels

4

design firm: MDG
art director: Mike Eaton
designer: Tim Merry (Creative Director)
client: MDG
software/hardware: Adobe Illustrator - MAC
paper/materials: Monadnock Astrolite Smooth
200 lb cover, laser cut,
debossed, and die-cut. 3-color
front. 1 color flood reverse.

1

MICHAEL GILLIS
founder, producer, director

10202 BRADDOCK DRIVE
CULVER CITY, CA 90232
323.816.6000 *tel*
310.876.8764 *fax*

MOGOMEDIA.COM
MGILLIS@MOGOMEDIA.COM

MOGOMEDIA

STRATEGIC STORYTELLING FOR
AUDIO, VIDEO, FILM & DVD

2

	1		2		3
design firm:	Cinquino + Co.	design firm:	Evenson Design	design firm:	MINE™
art director:	Ania J. Murray	art director:	Stan Evenson	art director:	Christopher Simmons
designer:	Ania J. Murray	designer:	Mark Sojka	designer:	Christopher Simmons
client:	Cinquino + Co.	client:	Mogomedia	client:	Steel Media
software/hardware:	Adobe Illustrator and InDesign	software/hardware:	EPS	software/hardware:	Adobe Illustrator CS2, Adobe InDesign CS2
paper/materials:	Embossed logo			paper/materials:	Finch Bright White Smooth 130 lb cover, Fasson Softcream 70 lb

3

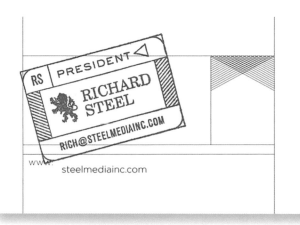

ACCOUNT MANAGER
SARA ★ ROSSINI
SARA@STEELMEDIAINC.COM

WWW: steelmediainc.com

STEEL MEDIA

49 West 69th Street, Suite 2A	NYC
TEL: 818 376 1399	NY 10023
FAX: 212 787 5016	

Like other firms, we know advertising. Unlike other firms, we know travel.	

RS | PRESIDENT
RICHARD STEEL
RICH@STEELMEDIAINC.COM

WWW: steelmediainc.com

STEEL MEDIA

49 West 69th Street, Suite 2A	NYC
TEL: 917 405 8590	NY 10023
FAX: 212 787 5016	

Like other firms, we know advertising. Unlike other firms, we know travel.	

ELISE@STEELMEDIAINC.COM
ELISE CARLSON
ACCT. MGR.

WWW: steelmediainc.com

STEEL MEDIA

49 West 69th Street, Suite 2A	NYC
TEL: 818 376 1399	NY 10023
FAX: 212 787 5016	

Like other firms, we know advertising. Unlike other firms, we know travel.	

JEN HODDEVIK
ACCOUNT MGR.
JEN@STEELMEDIAINC.COM

WWW: steelmediainc.com

STEEL MEDIA

49 West 69th Street, Suite 2A	NYC
TEL: 315 415 0070	NY 10023
FAX: 212 787 5016	

Like other firms, we know advertising. Unlike other firms, we know travel.	

evolutions

Berners Street
Soho Square
Oxford Street
Wells Street

Clare Buttress
Marketing Manager

T   020 7580 3333
M 07985 303 034
clare@evolutions.tv

www.evolutions.tv

evolutions

Berners Street
Soho Square
Oxford Street
Wells Street

Clare Buttress
Marketing Manager

T   020 7580 3333
M 07985 303 034
clare@evolutions.tv

www.evolutions.tv

evolutions

Berners Street
Soho Square
Oxford Street
Wells Street

Clare Buttress
Marketing Manager

T   020 7580 3333
M 07985 303 034
clare@evolutions.tv

www.evolutions.tv

evolutions

Berners Street
Soho Square
Oxford Street
Wells Street

Clare Buttress
Marketing Manager

T   020 7580 3333
M 07985 303 034
clare@evolutions.tv

www.evolutions.tv

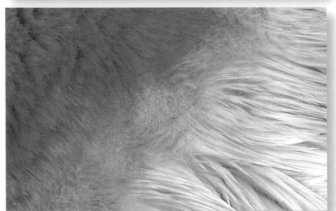

DUBLIN : LONDON : MANCHESTER
5 Schoolhouse Lane, Dublin 2, Ireland.
T: +353 (0)1 663 6400 **F**: +353 (0)1 663 6401

WWW.HKRARCHITECTS.COM

———

D: +353 (0)1 663 6480
M: +353 (0)87 691 1915
E: cgraefe@hkrarchitects.com

H<R ARCHITECTS

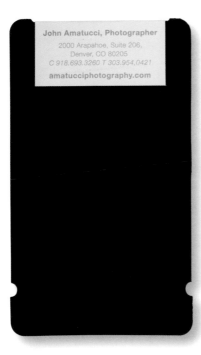

1

design firm: **Salterbaxter**
client: **Evolutions**
software/hardware: **Tiff**

2

design firm: **Detail Design Studio**
art director: **Detail Design Studio**
designer: **Detail Design Studio**
client: **HKR Architects**
software/hardware: **Adobe Illustrator and Quark Xpress**
paper/materials: **Arcoprint**

3

design firm: **David Clark Design**
art director: **David Clark**
designer: **Becky Gelder**
client: **Amatucci Photography**
software/hardware: **Adobe Illustrator CS**
paper/materials: **Touche Black cover, Fasson Crack and Peel**
printing: **Western Printing**

1

XANTHE matychak
ehtnax@yahoo.com > 607 342 2269

2

THOMAS
WOOD PRODUCTS

WILLIAM E. THOMAS

{610}777-6352

174 BRAN ROAD, SINKING SPRING, PENNSYLVANIA

POINTED STAKES, LUMBER, SEASONED FIREWOOD, CUSTOM SAWING

{mail} 33 S. 24th St. Mt. Penn, PA 19606

MOREBARN

{ ARTIST & PRODUCER MANAGEMENT }

GARY WALDMAN | 212.777.0611

GARY@MOREBARN.COM

628 BROADWAY SUITE 502

NEW YORK / NEW YORK / 10012

"I ONCE WENT DOWN TO NEIL YOUNG'S RANCH
AND HE ROWED ME OUT INTO THE MIDDLE OF A LAKE
(PUTTING MY LIFE IN HIS HANDS ONCE AGAIN).
He waved at someone invisible
and music started to play, in the countryside.
I REALIZED NEIL HAD HIS HOUSE WIRED AS THE LEFT SPEAKER,
AND HIS BARN WIRED AS THE RIGHT SPEAKER.
And Elliot Mazer, his engineer, said 'How is it?'
AND NEIL SHOUTED BACK: 'MORE BARN!'"
— GRAHAM NASH

GRASSCUTTERS

Arnie & Treston Clark
2 Walker Road
Kennebunk, Maine

985-3167   229-6924   294-1034

1

design firm: The Human Race
art director: Xanthe Matychak
designer: Xanthe Matychak
client: Xanthe Matychak
software/hardware: Adobe InDesign
paper/materials: Rubber stamp, reused
paperboard packaging

2

design firm: Johnston Duffy
art director: Martin Duffy
designer: Martin Duffy
client: Thomas Wood Company
software/hardware: Adobe Illustrator and Photoshop
paper/materials: Wood Veneer

3

design firm: Nothing: Something: NY
art director: Kevin Landwehr
designer: Kevin Landwehr
and Devin Becker
client: Morebarn Artist and
Producer Management

4

design firm: Boxwood Press
art director: Cheryl L. Clark
designer: Cheryl L. Clark
client: Grasscutters
paper/materials: Colored STAPLES stock

RUSTY GEORGE CREATIVE

CHARLOTTE BOUTZ
ACCOUNT MANAGER

	EMAIL:	WEBSITE:
	CHARLOTTE@	RUSTYGEORGE.COM

ADDRESS	732 BROADWAY, SUITE NO. 302	TEL:	253 284 2140	COPYRIGHT © 2006 RUSTY GEORGE CREATIVE ALL RIGHTS RESERVED.
	TACOMA, WASHINGTON 98402	FAX:	253 284 2142	

RUSTY GEORGE
CREATIVE PRINCIPAL

	EMAIL:	WEBSITE:
	RUSTY@	RUSTYGEORGE.COM

ADDRESS	732 BROADWAY, SUITE NO. 302	TEL:	253 284 2140	COPYRIGHT © 2006 RUSTY GEORGE CREATIVE ALL RIGHTS RESERVED.
	TACOMA, WASHINGTON 98402	FAX:	253 284 2142	

COLLECT 'EM ALL

PRINT IS DEAD NIKE A CULT

"THE SECRET TO CREATIVITY IS KNOWING HOW TO HIDE YOUR SOURCES." —ALBERT EINSTEIN

Q. WHAT CAN A PIZZA DO THAT AN ARTIST CAN'T?
A. FEED A FAMILY OF FOUR

IDENTITY
DIGITAL
PACKAGING
ADVERTISING
CULTURE

art & de

David Bishop
Creative Director

FRONT MEDIA

richard@frontmedia.co.uk
www.frontmedia.co.uk
+44 (0)1621 890 220
+44 (0)7880 743 235

3

MATHIAS SCHAAB, Dipl.-Kfm. Medienwirtschaft

WEBRAUM

Agentur für interaktive Medien, Rosenthaler Str. 39, 10178 Berlin
Office 030 63 37 11 87, Fax 030 63 37 11 88, Mobil 0163 718 41 75
E-Mail schaab@webraum.de, Internet www.webraum.de

4

Naila Mall-Goodro, M.A.
PRESIDENT

19141 Stone Oak Parkway
Suite 104 #248
San Antonio, Texas 78258
T/F 830 438 5012
M 619 985 9932

ngoodro@calarusgroup.com
www.calarusgroup.com

CALARUS GROUP
Valuable. Strategic. Solutions.

CALARUS GROUP
VALUABLE. STRATEGIC. SOLUTIONS.

19141 Stone Oak Parkway
Suite 104 #248
San Antonio, Texas 78258
T/F 830 438 5012

www.calarusgroup.com

1

design firm: Rusty George Creative
art director: Rusty George
designer: Lance Kagey
client: Rusty George Creative
software/hardware: Adobe Illustrator
paper/materials: French Paper,
Durotone Butcher Blue

2

design firm: Frontmedia
art director: Neil Maidment
and David Bishop
designer: Neil Maidment
client: Frontmedia
software/hardware: Adobe Illustrator and InDesign
paper/materials: Arctic Munken Lynx

3

design firm: R975
art director: Marcel Kummerer
designer: Marcel Kummerer
client: Webraum

4

design firm: Murillo Design, Inc.
art director: Roland Murillo
designer: Roland Murillo
client: Calarus Group
paper/materials: Strathmore Ultimate White
100 lb cover

	1		2		3
design firm:	Miles Design	design firm:	Zande + Newman Design	design firm:	Design Religion
art director:	Josh Miles	art director:	Adam Newman	art director:	Greg Russell
designer:	Eric Folzenlogel	designer:	Adam Newman	designer:	Tim Corbyn
client:	Miles Design	client:	Zande + Newman	client:	Design Religion
software/hardware:	Adobe Illustrator	software/hardware:	Adobe InDesign	software/hardware:	Adobe InDesign

1

ANDREW JENKINSON
CREATIVE DIRECTOR / CO-FOUNDER
+44 (0) 7739 981 842 ANDREW@FOLK.UK.COM

Folk

FOLK CREATIVE MARKETING 2A LUKE STREET LONDON EC2A 4NT
T +44 (0) 207 739 8444 F +44 (0) 207 033 0018 W WWW.FOLK.UK.COM

MATT BUTTERWORTH
MANAGING DIRECTOR / CO-FOUNDER
+44 (0) 7740 738 556 MATT@FOLK.UK.COM

Folk

FOLK CREATIVE MARKETING 2A LUKE STREET LONDON EC2A 4NT
T +44 (0) 207 739 8444 F +44 (0) 207 033 0018 W WWW.FOLK.UK.COM

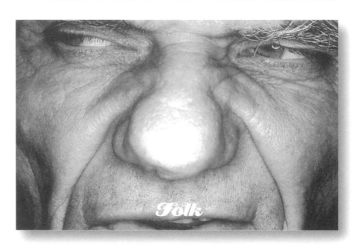

2

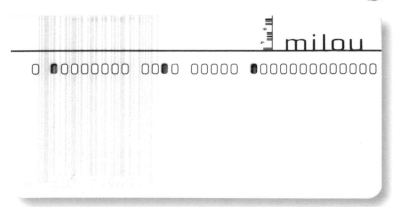

milou

14795 SW Murray Scholls Drive ... Suite 101 ... Beaverton, Oregon 97007

| APPOINTMENT | | 503 | 579 9600 – TEL |
| Date_____ Time_____ | | | 579 0857 – FAX |

T-BOX™

BILL GERMAN
BGERMAN@T-BOXINC.COM
TOLL FREE: 1.866.363.TBOX [8269]

5807 WEST 73ᴿᴰ STREET INDIANAPOLIS, IN 46278

| [T] 317.291.8269 | [F] 317.216.0735 | [M] 317.557.9146 |

IF IT'S GOLF, IT STARTS HERE.™
WWW.T-BOXINC.COM

1

design firm: Folk Creative Ltd.
art director: Andrew Jenkinson
designer: Andrew Jenkinson
client: Folk Creative Ltd.
software/hardware: Adobe InDesign and Photoshop
paper/materials: Uncoated 2-color Litho

2

design firm: Fangman Design
art director: Matt Fangman
designer: Matt Fangman
illustrator: Matt Fangman
client: Fangman Design
software/hardware: Adobe Illustrator
paper/materials: French Paper Durotone,
Butcher White 100 lb cover

3

design firm: Dotzero Design
designer: Karen Wippich and Jon Wippich
client: Davis Agency
software/hardware: Adobe Illustrator and Photoshop
paper/materials: Classic Crest

4

design firm: Miles Design
art director: Josh Miles
designer: Eric Folzenlogel
client: T-Box
software/hardware: Adobe Illustrator CS
paper/materials: Cougar White 100 lb

1

Patricia Tay Account Executive

7145 West Credit Ave, Building 1, Suite 102
Mississauga, Ontario L5N 6J7 Canada
T 905 603 0180 EXT.800 **F** 905 603 8180
C 416 993 7660 patricia@onemethod.com
www.onemethod.com

2

林赛 卡姆

创始人，副总裁

别忘了联络：

NAGTAGS

电话　415 454 7844
传真　415 454 7834
电子邮件　LINDSAY@NAGTAGS.COM
通讯地址　PO BOX 1058 LARKSPUR, CA 94977

lindsay kamm!

don't forget to:

NAGTAGS

call 415 454 7844
fax 415 454 7834
email LINDSAY@NAGTAGS.COM
write PO BOX 1058 LARKSPUR, CA 94977

vocal
consulting group

Diane Sheets
Vocal Consultant
Certified Master, EVTS

T: 877.263.8805
E: DIANESHEETS@VOCALCONSULTING.COM

COLUMBUS, OH / NASHVILLE, TN

3

WWW.VOCALCONSULTING.COM

turnstyle

4

Steve Watson
Principal / Design
22th NW Market Street
Seattle WA 98107
phone 206.297.7390
fax 206.297.7390
mobile 206.849.0122
steve.watson@turnstylestudio.com

ſ

1

design firm: Onemethod Inc.
art director: Amin Todai
designer: Ryan Saley
client: Onemethod Inc.
software/hardware: Adobe Illustrator
paper/materials: Centura

2

design firm: MINE™
art director: Christopher Simmons
designer: Christopher Simmons
and Kate Earhart
client: Nagtags
software/hardware: Adobe Illustrator CS2,
Adobe InDesign CS2
paper/materials: Mohawk Superfine Ultrawhite
Smooth 130 lb DTC

3

design firm: Element
art director: Megan Graham
designer: Megan Graham
client: Vocal Consulting Group
software/hardware: Adobe InDesign

4

design firm: Turnstyle
art director: Ben Graham, Steve Watson
designer: Steve Watson
client: Turnstyle
software/hardware: Adobe Illustrator
paper/materials: Fix River Starwhite
30 lb Double-thick Cover

Tequila Mockingbird
Music & Sound Design

Jeremiah Clifton
Engineer/Webmaster
jeremiah@tequilamockingbird.com
Mobile: 512-757-3808

306 West Sixteenth Street
Austin, Texas 78701
Phone: 512-499-8655
Fax: 512-499-8057
tequilamockingbird.com

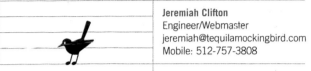

2

3

PHILIP NAUDÉ
philip@24hourplays.com
Cell: 917.892.8290

www.24hourplays.com

b:løk

BLOK DESIGN | VANESSA ARRIOJA | T: [52 55] 55 15 24 23

SOMBRERETE 515-1 CONDESA MEXICO DF 06170 | va@blokdesign.com

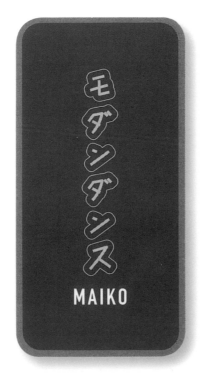

2

PATRICK CHIU

311 W. 6TH STREET
AUSTIN TEXAS 78701
MAIKOAUSTIN.COM

(p) 512 236 9888
(c) 832 876 1688
(f) 512 236 9889

TIMOTHY ROLLINS
MANAGING PARTNER

METROPOLITAN PARTNERS
150 EAST BROAD STREET COLUMBUS, OHIO 43215
614.883.1300 FAX: 614.221.1380
TROLLINS@METROPOLITANPARTNERS.INFO
A LIMITED LIABILITY COMPANY

3

cdk
PARTNERS

michelle libonati
executive assistant
michelle@cdkpartners.com
602/258/1222 fax 602/258/4541
2 north central ave. suite 1100
phoenix, az 85004

4

cdkpartners.com

1

design firm: Blok
art director: Vanessa Eckstein
designer: Vanessa Eckstein
client: Blok
software/hardware: Adobe Illustrator
paper/materials: Strathmore Ultimate White

2

design firm: Foda Studio
art director: Jett Butler
designer: Jett Butler
client: Maiko Japanese Restaurant
software/hardware: Adobe Illustrator
paper/materials: Neenah Classic Laid
Natural White 120 lb cover

3

design firm: Scott Adams Design Associates
designer: Scott Adams
client: Metropolitan Partners
software/hardware: Quark Xpress
paper/materials: Neenah Classic Crest

4

design firm: Campbell Fisher Design
art director: Greg Fisher
designer: Stacy Crawford
client: CDK Partners
software/hardware: Adobe Illustrator
paper/materials: Classic Crest 165 lb cover

1

2

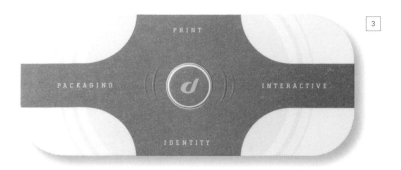

DPD STUDIO | 2908 OREGON COURT SUITE I-12 | TORRANCE CA 90503

3

4

1

design firm: Root Idea
art director: Ken Lee
designer: Ken Lee
client: Root Idea
software/hardware: Photoshop and Adobe Illust
paper/materials: Antalis, soft touch

2

design firm: Campbell Fisher Design
art director: Mike Campbell
designer: Stacy Crawford
client: Alchemy
software/hardware: Adobe Illustrator
paper/materials: Domtar Solutions
Cararra White 100 lb cover

3

design firm: dpd studio
art director: Dennis Purcell
designer: Dennis Purcell
client: dpd studio
software/hardware: Adobe Illustrator
paper/materials: French Paper Company
Smart White

4

design firm: dpd studio
art director: Dennis Purcell
designer: Dennis Purcell
client: JNR8
software/hardware: Adobe Illustrator

1

KIRK ROARK

220 N. Zapata Hwy. #11
Laredo, TX 78043
U.S. phone 469-361-2309
kroark@zaragozavineyards.com

Aldama #3 C.P. 37700
San Miguel de Allende, GTO
mobile 044-415-100-3788
kroark@zaragozavineyards.com

2

GRAPHIC DESIGN
ADVERTISING
ILLUSTRATION
IDENTITY
WEB DESIGN
ENVIRONMENTAL
PACKAGING
TEXTILE
EVENTS

KO-EST. 78

3

kopsa otte™
Certified Public Accountants & Advisors

Katie Stoll

Katherine Stoll
kstoll@kopsaotte.com

EXT-118

306 East Seventh St.   T. (402)362.6636
York, NE 68467 U.S.A.   F. (402)362.5475

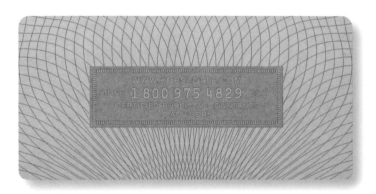

WWW.KOPSAOTTE.COM
TF.No. 1 800 975 4829 U.S.A.
CERTIFIED PUBLIC ACCOUNTANTS
& ADVISORS

We:Do!
WEDDING PHOTOGRAPHY
& concept solutions

4

DIMITRA DELI
_CREATIVE

Κηφισίας 236
145 62 ΚΗΦΙΣΙΑ
Εμπ. Κέντρο "Αίγλη"
1ος όροφος

Tel/Fax: 210 80 15 362
ΚΙΝ. 6942 05 32 59
info@we-do.gr
www.we-do.gr

1
design firm: Sibley Peteet Design—Dallas
art director: Don Sibley
designer: Brandon Kirk
client: Zaragoza Vineyards
software/hardware: Adobe Illustrator

2
design firm: Haute Haus Creative
art director: Don Lewis
designer: Don Lewis
client: Haute Haus Creative
software/hardware: Freehand and Quark Xpress
paper/materials: Classic Crest, scored, glued

3
design firm: Archrival
art director: Joel Kreutzer
designer: Joel Kreutzer
client: Kopsa Otte
software/hardware: Adobe Illustrator CS2

4
design firm: Di Depux
art director: Despina Bournele
designer: Despina Bournele
client: Constantinos Delis and Demitra
software/hardware: Adobe Illustrator CS
paper/materials: 3 Pantone, Curious 250 gsm

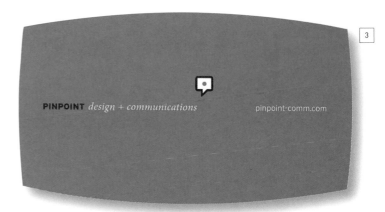

1	2	3
design firm: **Trade Creative Services**	design firm: **Joe Shouldice Design**	design firm: **Pinpoint Communications**
art director: **Jay Rogers**	art director: **Joe Shouldice**	art director: **James Kluetz and Paul Cooper**

1

Baseman Design Associates
221 Mather Road
Jenkintown, Pennsylvania 19046 **USA**

BDA

Frank Baseman   t. 215 885 7157
frank@basemandesign.com   f. 215 885 7156
www.basemandesign.com

2

JEFF BREAZEALE PARTNER

3 1 1 6 MAIN STREET, DALLAS, TEXAS 75226
jeff@matchboxstudio.com

PHONE 214 939 3100

FAX 214 939 3400

FY2K
Modern Furniture
Collections

4 Foster Street Surry Hills NSW 2010
T +61 2 9281 1771 F +61 2 9281 1774
julie@fy2k.com.au
www.fy2k.com.au

Julie Angland

3

canvas

4

1

design firm: Baseman Design Associates
art director: Frank Baseman
designer: Frank Baseman
client: Baseman Design Associates
software/hardware: Quark Xpress
paper/materials: Crane's 130 lb cover
letterpress printing

2

design firm: The Matchbox Studio
art director: Jeff Breazeale and Liz Burnett
designer: Jeff Breazeale and Liz Burnett
client: The Matchbox Studio
paper/materials: Classic Cotton Bristol
Solar White cover

3

design firm: There
art director: There
designer: There
client: FY2K
software/hardware: Adobe Illustrator
paper/materials: Various

4

design firm: JSDS
art director: JSDS
designer: Justin Skeesuck
client: JSDS
software/hardware: Adobe Illustrator
paper/materials: Vintage postcard
letterpress

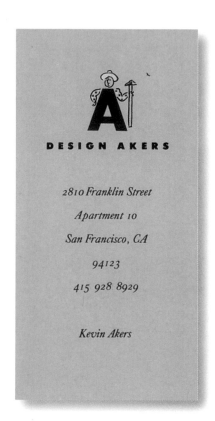

DESIGN AKERS

2810 Franklin Street

Apartment 10

San Francisco, CA

94123

415 928 8929

Kevin Akers

1

2

1441 EAST PENDER STREET, VANCOUVER
BRITISH COLUMBIA, V5L1V7 CANADA
FACSIMILE 604 669 2010 _ www.battersbyhowat.com

BETTINA BALCAEN
604 669 9647 _ bettina@battersbyhowat.com

BATTERSBY
HOWAT

3

NOTHING: SOMETHING: NY

A VISUAL AGENCY

TELE

646-221-9972

MAIL

WHATISIT@NOTHINGSOMETHING.COM

KEVIN LANDWEHR   718•[3887840]

4

242 WYTHE AVENUE, STUDIO #3
BROOKLYN, NEW YORK, 11211

WWW.NOTHINGSOMETHING.COM

1

design firm: Kevin Akers Design and Image
art director: Kevin Akers
designer: Kevin Akers
illustrator: Kevin Akers
client: Kevin Akers
software/hardware: Adobe Illustrator
paper/materials: Simpson

2

design firm: Subplot Design, Inc.
art director: Roy White, Matthew Clark
designer: Steph Gibson
client: Battersbyhowat Architects
software/hardware: Adobe Illustrator
paper/materials: Curious Touch,
Mohawk Superfine

3

design firm: Flipcide
art director: Roy Dequina
designer: Roy Dequina
client: Xplosiv Training
software/hardware: Adobe Illustrator
paper/materials: TopKote Uncoated 110 lb

4

design firm: Nothing: Something: NY
art director: Kevin Landwehr
designer: Kevin Landwehr
and Devin Becker
client: Nothing: Something: NY
paper/materials: Neenah Classic Crest 130 lb

1

design firm: Art Institute of Orange County
art director: Maggie Rassoni, MFA

EMIGRE FILM

Nassar Design / 11 Park Street
Suite 1 / Brookline MASS. 02446
T 617 264.2862   F 617 264.2861
n.nassar@verizon.net

Nélida Nassar

3

City Centre Ventures
Suite 201 - 1300 First Avenue
Prince George, BC V2L 2Y3
www.citycentreventures.com

t: (250) 649 3204
f: (250) 649 3200
c: (250) 552 9537
e: lachman@initiativespg.com

4

KATHY
LACHMAN

1

design firm: Blok
art director: Vanessa Eckstein
designer: Vanessa Eckstein,
Mariana Contegni,
Patricia Kleeberg
client: Émigré Film
software/hardware: Adobe Illustrator
paper/materials: Fox River Sirius Smooth

2

design firm: Matthew Schwartz
Design Studio
art director: Matthew Schwartz
client: Speedy Fixit
software/hardware: Adobe Illustrator
and InDesign

3

design firm: Nassar Design
art director: Nélida Nassar
designer: Nélida Nassar
client: Nassar Design
software/hardware: Quark Xpress
paper/materials: Curious Metallic Anodized,
1 color

4

design firm: smashLAB
art director: Eric Karjaluoto
designer: Javier Plug
illustrator: Javier Plug
client: City Centre Ventures
software/hardware: Adobe Illustrator
paper/materials: Save-A-Tree 100 lb cover

Shirts for people.

This business is located at
8220 La Mirada Place, Suite 500,
Albuquerque, New Mexico, 87109.
The phone number is 505.293.2333.
The email is info@sackwear.com.

100% Funny Shirts.
Wear daily. Do not bleach.
Tumble dry low.

Made in the USA

Shirts for people.

This business is located at
20 La Mirada Place, Suite 500,
uquerque, New Mexico, 87109.
hone number is 505.293.2333.
mail is info@sackwear.com.

2

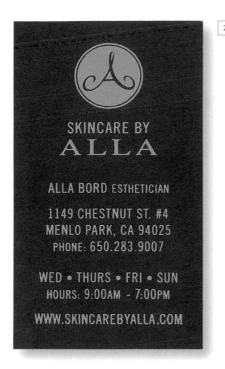

3

1

design firm: 3
art director: Sam Maclay
designer: Tim McGrath
illustrator: Tim McGrath
client: Sackwear.com
software/hardware: Quark Xpress
and Adobe Illustrator
paper/materials: French Paper, with neck tags
stitched in; Rubber stamps

2

design firm: Sandy Gin Design
designer: Sandy Gin
client: Skincare by Alla
software/hardware: Macromedia Freehand
paper/materials: Speckletone 100 lb cover,
Foil Stamped

3

design firm: Dotzero Design
designer: Karen Wippich and Jon Wippich
client: Davis Agency
paper/materials: Classic Crest Natural White

1

THE GLOBAL LEGAL PLATFORM
www.serengetilaw.com

SERENGETI

GREG SHRIBER
Project Manager

T +1.425.748.5115
F +1.425.748.5116
E greg.shriber@serengetilaw.com

2018 156th Ave. NE
Suite No. 100
Bellevue, WA 98007

2

AMY JENKINS
amy@stickirice.com

sticki rice

1222 EAST BLVD
CHARLOTTE NC 28203
(p) 704.644.5363   (f) 704.248.8487

GIFTS | ACCENTS | HOME DECOR

sticki rice

WWW.STICKIRICE.COM

PERBACCO

ristorante + bar

www.perbaccosf.com

230 California Street
San Francisco, CA 94111

tel   415-955-0663
fax   415-955-0676

3

KATIE NEILL

KATIE@800HIGHSTREET.COM

800 HIGH STREET

PALO ALTO, CA 94301

650.863.9800

800HIGHSTREET.COM

4

1

design firm: **Turnstyle**
art director: **Steve Watson**
designer: **Steve Watson**
client: **Serengeti**
software/hardware: **Adobe Illustrator**
paper/materials: **Fox River Starwhite Tiar**
Vellum 130 lb DTC

2

design firm: **Ginger Griffin Marketin**
and Design
art director: **Kara Hollinger**
designer: **Kara Hollinger**
client: **Sticki Rice**
software/hardware: **Adobe Illustrator CS2**
paper/materials: **Mohawk Navajo 100 lb,**
custom die-cut

3

design firm: **Bakken Creative Co.**
art director: **Michelle Bakken**
designer: **Tae Hatayama**
client: **Perbacco Ristorante an**
software/hardware: **Adobe Illustrator**

4

design firm: **Bakken Creative Co.**
art director: **Michelle Bakken**
designer: **Gina Mondello**
client: **Pacific Marketing Asso**
software/hardware: **Adobe Illustrator**

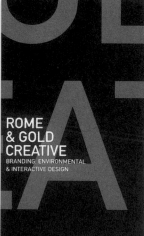

ROME
& GOLD
CREATIVE

LORENZO ROMERO, PRINCIPAL

PH. 505.897.0870
FX. 505.843.7500

LORENZO@RGCREATIVE.COM

1606 CENTRAL AVE. SE SUITE 102
ALBUQUERQUE, NM 87106

WWW.RGCREATIVE.COM

2

3

1		2		3	
design firm:	Rome & Gold Creative	design firm:	WOW Branding	design firm:	Mingovits
art director:	Robert Goldie	art director:	Perry Chua	client:	Aaron Niemi, LMT

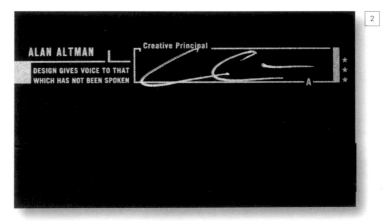

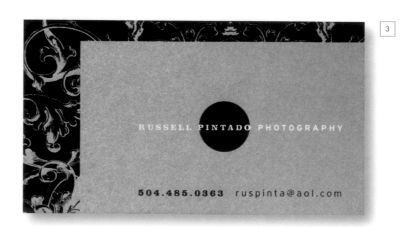

4

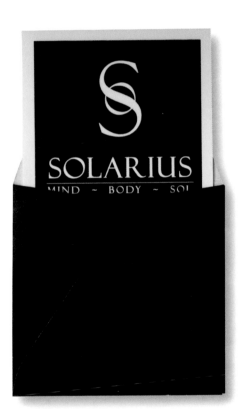

SOLARIUS
MIND ~ BODY ~ SOL

SOLARIUS
MIND ~ BODY ~ SOL

1

design firm: Switch Creative
art director: Michael Carpenter
designer: Michael Carpenter
client: Vaughn the workshop
software/hardware: Adobe Illustrator
paper/materials: Silk cards and foil

2

design firm: A3 Design
art director: Amanda Altman
designer: Alan Altman
client: A3 Design
software/hardware: Adobe Illustrator

3

design firm: Louviere + Vanessa
art director: Jeff Louviere
designer: Jeff Louviere
client: Russell Pintado Photography
software/hardware: Adobe Illustrator and Photosh
paper/materials: 2-color on Mohawk

4

design firm: Rome & Gold Creative
art director: Lorenzo Romero
designer: Robert Goldie
client: Solarius
software/hardware: Adobe Illustrator
paper/materials: Neenah Classic Crest Natural
Super Smooth 80 lb cover

1

KYEONG-WON YOUN

•

Art Director/Graphic Designer

•

7070 Grelot Rd #138
Mobile, AL 36695

•

251.776.7572(H)
251.461.1437(O)

•

kwyoun@hotmail.com
www.southalabama.edu/art/

2

mobile_551.998.6446
email_george@georgefontenette.com

1

design firm: YOUN Graphic and
Interactive Design
art director: Kyeong-Won Youn
designer: Kyeong-Won Youn
client: YOUN Graphic and
Interactive Design
software/hardware: Adobe Illustrator

2

design firm: 3rd Edge Communications
art director: Frankie Gonzalez
designer: Nick Schmitz
client: George Fontenette

3

design firm: Dot 1 Design
art director: Bruno Catanho
designer: Bruno Catanho
client: Dot 1 Design
software/hardware: Adobe Illustrator
paper/materials: Metal FX Spot Colour on 250 lb
card with static case covers

3

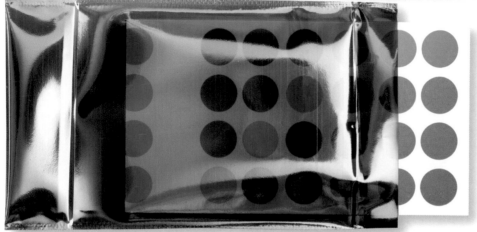

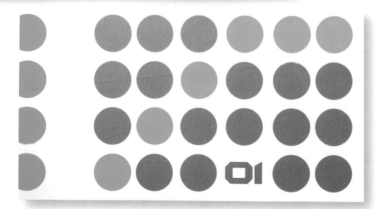

B C

M D

OI

tel: 07967672140
binda, sales & new media development consultant
www.dot1design.co.uk e-mail: binda@dot1design.co.uk

1

Jorge Toro
Asst General Manager

500 N Water Street
Corpus Christi, TX 78471
p 361 882 5552
f 361 882 5555
www.havanacc.com

HAVANA

1

design firm: MBA
art director: Mark Brinkman and Mike Coffin

2

design firm: Orangeseed Design
art director: Damien Wolf

3

design firm: Fuel
designer: Bill Bollman, Lance Lethcoe,

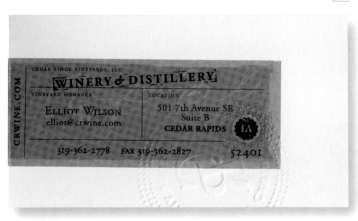

DRY™ www.drysoda.com

SODA CO: SHARELLE KLAUS / FOUNDER & CEO
T/F 253.573.0197 / **M** 253.970.8201 / **E** sharelle@drysoda.com
715 North J Street / Tacoma, WA 98403

2

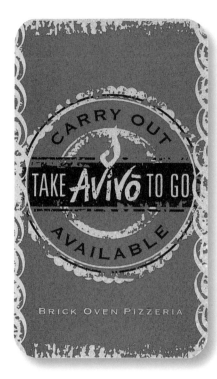

CARRY OUT
TAKE *Avivō* TO GO
AVAILABLE
BRICK OVEN PIZZERIA

3

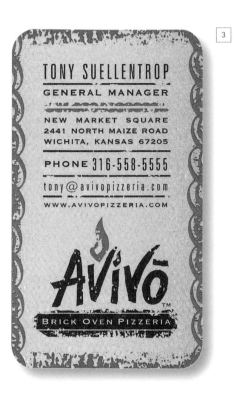

TONY SUELLENTROP
GENERAL MANAGER
NEW MARKET SQUARE
2441 NORTH MAIZE ROAD
WICHITA, KANSAS 67205
PHONE 316-558-5555
tony@avivopizzeria.com
WWW.AVIVOPIZZERIA.COM

Avivō™
BRICK OVEN PIZZERIA

4

WWW.JASMINEBLACK.COM   JASMINEBLACKPAPER@YAHOO.COM

Jasmine black
PAPER + GIFT

| JENNIFER BLACK | 3703 KERBEY LANE, AUSTIN 78731 | JASON SCHUBERT |
| | 512 420-2680   TO FAX JUST ADD 1 | |

1

design firm: Design Ranch
art director: Michelle Sonderegger
& Ingrid Sidie
designer: Michelle Sonderegger
client: Nine Lives
software/hardware: Adobe Illustrator

2

design firm: Turnstyle
art director: Steve Watson
designer: Steve Watson
client: Dry Soda
software/hardware: Adobe Illustrator
paper/materials: Fox River Starwhite Tiara
Vellum 130 lb DTC

3

design firm: Entermotion Design Studio
designer: Lea Morrow
client: Avivo Brick Oven Pizza and
In the Sauce Brands
software/hardware: Macromedia Freehand
paper/materials: Domtar Feltweave, 3 color

4

design firm: Shoehorn
designer: Will Hornaday
client: Jasmine Black Paper and Gift
software/hardware: Adobe Illustrator CS
paper/materials: Classic Crest Windsor Blue
80 lb cover

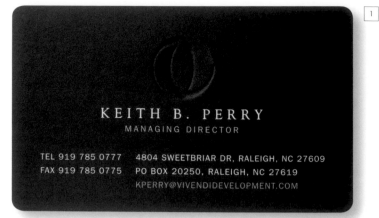

1

2

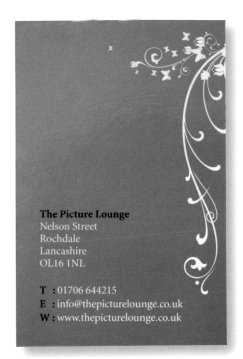

3

The Picture Lounge
Nelson Street
Rochdale
Lancashire
OL16 1NL

T : 01706 644215
E : info@thepicturelounge.co.uk
W : www.thepicturelounge.co.uk

4

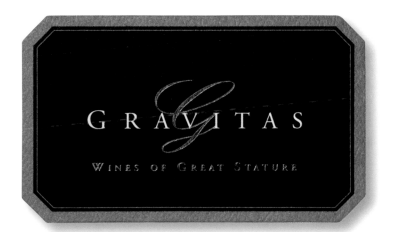

PETER KERDEMELIDIS
Vineyard Manager

FROM SAINT ARNAUD'S VINEYARD

Lanark Lane (off State Highway 63), Wairau Valley, Marlborough, New Zealand
PO Box 23, Renwick, Marlborough, New Zealand
Tel: +64 (0) 3 572 2731, Mobile: +64 (0) 27 459 273, Fax: +64 (0) 3 572 2732
Email: vineyard@new-zealand-wines.com www.new-zealand-wines.com

GRAVITAS

WINES OF GREAT STATURE

1

design firm: Helena Seo Design
art director: Helena Seo
designer: Helena Seo
client: Vivendi Development
software/hardware: Adobe Illustrator
paper/materials: Starwhite Sirius Smooth
130 lb DTC

2

design firm: Murillo Design, Inc.
art director: Roland Murillo
designer: Roland Murillo
client: Iungo Arts Magazine
paper/materials: Mohawk Superfine Eggshell
White 120 DTC

3

design firm: Creative Spark
art director: Art director: Andy Mallalieu
designer: Andy Mallalieu
client: The Picture Lounge/ Jamilla Paul
software/hardware: Adobe Illustrator
paper/materials: 300 gsm, silk paper,
high gloss finish,
metallic gold ink

4

design firm: Lloyds Graphic Design Ltd.
art director: Alexander Lloyd
designer: Alexander Lloyd
client: Gravitas
software/hardware: Macromedia Freehand
paper/materials: Sundance Ultrawhite 270 gsm

1

 success by design Limb Design

Elise De Silva

Principal

7026 Old Katy Road - Suite 350
Houston, Texas 77024

tel 713 529 1117   cell 713 703 7624

elise@limbdesign.com
www.limbdesign.com

2

ARRINGTON
PHOTOGRAPHY

Elizabeth Arrington
www.arringtonphotography.net
info@arringtonphotography.net
512.468.5661

Photo Journalism · Advertising · Weddings · Graduations · Portraits
On Location · Studio · B&W · Color

Julie Challman
Software Engineer

Parametric™
Leaders in Structured Portfolio Management

1151 Fairview Avenue North
Seattle, WA 98109-4418

T 206 694 5516
F 206 694 5566
E jchallman@paraport.com

www.parametricportfolio.com

KEVIN AKERS

13 HART STREET

SAN RAFAEL, CA

ZIP 94901-2605

HOME 415.459.3424

STUDIO 415.455.0562

FAX 415.455.0597

MODEM 415.459.4767

1

design firm: Limb Design
art director: Emilie Gruson
designer: Emilie Gruson
client: Limb Design
software/hardware: Adobe InDesign
paper/materials: Mohawk Superfine

2

design firm: Lolight Design
art director: Aaron Deckler
designer: Aaron Deckler
client: Arrington Photography
software/hardware: Adobe Photoshop and InDesig

3

design firm: Turnstyle
art director: Ben Graham
designer: Jason Gomez
client: Parametric
software/hardware: Adobe Illustrator
paper/materials: Mohawk Strathmore Ultimate
White 110 lb cover

4

design firm: Kevin Akers Design and Image
art director: Kevin Akers
designer: Kevin Akers
illustrator: Kevin Akers
client: Kevin Akers
software/hardware: Adobe Illustrator

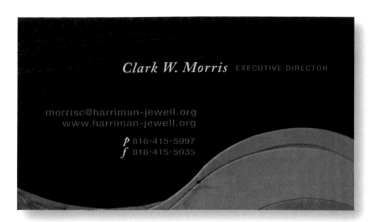

Clark W. Morris   EXECUTIVE DIRECTOR

morrisc@harriman-jewell.org
www.harriman-jewell.org
p 816·415·5997
f 816·415·5035

Harriman-Jewell Series

William Jewell College
500 College Hill, Campus Box 1015
Liberty, Missouri 64068-1896

Dale B.
MANAGING

45 ROCKEFELLER P
NEW YORK, NEW YORK 10111

telephone _____ 212 **332.1112**   *facsimile* _____ 212 **332.1113**

email __ DCHAPPELL@BLACKHORSECAP.COM

BLACK HORSE
Capital

1		2		3	
design firm:	Design Center, Ltd.	design firm:	BR	design firm:	A3 Design
art director:	Eduard Cehovin	art director:	Nathaniel Cooper	art director:	Amanda Altman
designer:	Eduard Cehovin	designer:	Nathaniel Cooper	designer:	Alan Altman

FIONA GUY ACIPR

E • fiona@impactmediapr.com
M • 07974 722275

MM2 Building • 84 Pickford Street
Manchester • M4 5BT

T • +44 (0) 161 236 0008
F • +44 (0) 161 236 0204
W • www.impactmediapr.com

1

design firm: **Creative Spark**

art director: **Neil Marra**

designer: **Andy Mallalieu**

client: **Impact Media PR**

software/hardware: **Adobe Illustrator and Photoshop**

paper/materials: **300 gsm, matte laminated,**
spot-varnished

2

design firm: **Home**

art director: **Ben Hickman**

designer: **Ben Hickman**

client: **Home**

software/hardware: **Adobe Illustrator**
and Quark Xpress

paper/materials: **400 gsm Mellotex,**
Matt Lam and Spot UV

3

design firm: **Willoughby Design Group**

art director: **Nate Hardin and Anne Simmons**
(Creative director)

designer: **Nate Hardin**

client: **Links Fitness**

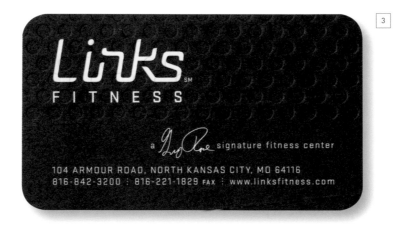

Ben Hickman Creative Director
a: 71 fleetwood avenue   westcliff on sea   essex   ss0 9rb
phone home: +44 (0)1702 344692   m: +44 (0)7703 444764
e: info@homecreatives.com   w: www.homecreatives.com

2

3

a signature fitness center
104 ARMOUR ROAD, NORTH KANSAS CITY, MO 64116
816-842-3200 : 816-221-1829 FAX : www.linksfitness.com

dvaughan@linksfitness.com

DOUG VAUGHAN
CHIEF EXECUTIVE OFFICER
913-638-3542 MOBILE

1

2

3

1

design firm: Think Studio, NYC
art director: John Clifford
designer: John Clifford
client: Soulpicnic Interactive
software/hardware: Adobe Illustrator
and Quark Xpress
paper/materials: Mohawk Superfine

2

design firm: Campbell Fisher Design
art director: Greg Fisher
designer: Stacy Crawford
and Ashley Flanagan
client: Champ Car
software/hardware: Adobe Illustrator
paper/materials: Classic Crest 165 lb cover

3

design firm: Base Art Co.
art director: Terry Rohrbach
designer: Terry Rohrbach
client: Base Art Co.
software/hardware: Adobe InDesign
paper/materials: Acrylic

1

AUBURN RIDGE

Finely Crafted Kitchens, Cabinets, and Millwork

BOB RENFORTH
CABINET AND MILLWORK SPECIALIST

2424 RIMROCK ROAD   TEL   866/473/4925
MADISON, WI 53713   CELL   608/209/4163
BRENFORTH@AUBURNRIDGE.COM   FAX   608/655/3553

WWW.AUBURNRIDGE.COM

2

Morrow & Co. LLC
CERTIFIED PUBLIC ACCOUNTANTS

Richard L. Morrow CPA
PHONE 316.263.2223   FAX 316.263.2302
421 EAST 3RD STREET NORTH ▪ WICHITA, KS 67202
E rich@morrowandcompany.com

ACCOUNTING FOR YOUR NEEDS℠
www.morrowandcompany.com

3

TM

TRADEMARK™
PACKAGING
A Division of First Pacific Enterprises Inc.

E steve@trademarkpackaging.com   TF 1 888 545 3090
T 250 545 3098   F 250 545 3239   C 250 212 9094
W www.trademarkpackaging.com

STEVE HARVEY
NATIONAL SALES MGR.

Our Packaging is your Trademark™

CANADA Suite 600, 280 Nelson St, Vancouver, BC V6B 2E2
USA 305 North Harbor Blvd, San Pedro, CA 90731

CANADA
USA

4

THE
DESIGN FIRM

Luke Despatie

One Vancouver Avenue, Toronto, ON M4L 2S7
416.995.0243   luke@thedesignfirm.ca

www.thedesignfirm.ca

1

design firm: Shine Advertising
art director: Mike Kriefski, John Krull
designer: Emilie Smith
client: Auburn Ridge

2

design firm: Entermotion Design Studio
designer: Lea Morrow
client: Morrow and Company
software/hardware: Macromedia Freehand

3

design firm: Dossier Creative, Inc.
art director: Don Chisholm
designer: Patrick Smith
client: Trademark Packaging
software/hardware: Adobe Illustrator and InDesign
paper/materials: Mohawk Navajo Brilliant White
120 lb cover

4

design firm: The Design Firm
art director: Luke Despatie
designer: Luke Despatie
client: The Design Firm
software/hardware: Quark Xpress
paper/materials: Neenah Classic Crest

1

design firm: Design Ranch
art director: Michelle Sonderegger
and Igred Sidie
designer: Ted Carpenter and Rachel Karaca
client: Bennett Schneider
software/hardware: Adobe Illustrator .

bennett schneider
specialty greetings & paper

merikay lott

loc 311 east 55th street _ kansas city, missouri 64113

tele 816.444.8484 _ mail ml@bennettschneider.com

fax 816.444.3115 _ web bennettschneider.com

bennett schneider
specialty greetings & paper

loc 311 east 55th street _ kansas city, missouri 64113

tele 816.444.8484 _ mail info@bennettschneider.com

fax 816.444.3115 _ web bennettschneider.com

bennett schneider
specialty greetings & paper

Randy Sorrell
randy@choosesurroundings.com

t 317.575.0482
f 317.575.9818
choosesurroundings.com

421 South Rangeline Rd.
Carmel, IN 46032

SURROUNDINGS
BY NATUREWORKS+

design firm: **Miles Design**

art director: **Josh Miles**

designer: **Eric Folzenlogel**

client: **Surroundings**

software/hardware: **Adobe Illustrator CS2**

paper/materials: **Cougar 100 lb Cover,**
die-cut offset, foil emboss

design firm: **Ginger Griffin**
Marketing and Design

art director: **Kara Hollinger**

designer: **Eddy Herty and Kara Hollinger**

client: **Ginger Griffin**
Marketing and Design

software/hardware: **Adobe Illustrator CS**

paper/materials: **Cranes Fluorescent White**

design firm: **Sheriff Design**

art director: **Paul Sheriff**

designer: **Paul Sheriff**

client: **Patti Dougherty**

3

215/635/2381
sparkypd@comcast.net

7703 Union Avenue
Elkins Park, PA
19027-2645

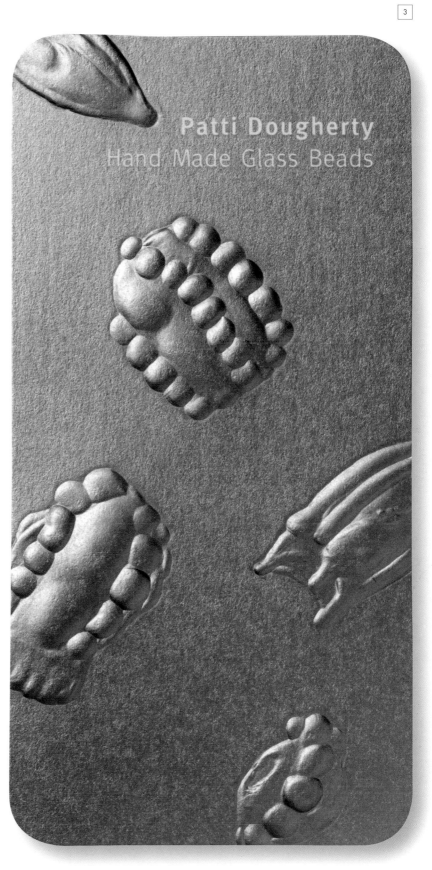

Patti Dougherty
Hand Made Glass Beads

1

2

Tina Jukić Tomljanović

SAPIO
J. Vogrinca 18, 10000 Zagreb
tel/fax: (01) 3833-193
info@ulola.com, www.ulola.com

ULOLA   PRIRODNI KOZMETIČKI PROIZVODI

Eina McHugh
Director

11a Eustace Street, Temple Bar, Dublin 2. Ireland.
t. +353 1 635 7202 f. +353 1 670 7758 e. eina@ark.ie
www.ark.ie

The Ark
A Cultural Centre for Children
Lárionad Cultúir na Leanaí

1

design firm: Imagine
art director: David Caunce
designer: David Caunce
client: Pastiche
software/hardware: Adobe Illustrator
paper/materials: 300 gsm, matte, lamination

2

design firm: smashLAB
art director: Eric Karjaluoto
designer: Peter Pimentel
illustrator: Peter Pimentel
client: Frogfile Office Essentials
software/hardware: Adobe Illustrator
paper/materials: Vegetable-based inks,
processed chlorine-free
100% post-consumer waste
Save-A-Tree paper

3

design firm: Elevator
art director: Tony Adamic
designer: Tony Adamic and Lana Vitas
client: Ulola
software/hardware: Adobe Illustrator
paper/materials: Conqueror Stonemarquee

4

design firm: Detail Design Studio
art director: Detail Design Studio
designer: Detail Design Studio
client: The Ark:
A Cultural Centre for Children
software/hardware: Adobe Illustrator
and Quark Xpress
paper/materials: Splendorgel

1

THE
katalyst
CONSULTANCY

→ kevin carroll, katalyst
503.807.2401

pmb 341 • 9220 sw barbur blvd • #119
portland, oregon • 97219
kc@katalystconsultancy.com

68   8
                                      06
Dr⁺   4
                                      04
Dreamer   14
199.1109   1

2

SPI
HOME

377 SWIFT AVENUE, SOUTH SAN FRANCISCO, CA 94080
WWW.SPI-HOME.COM

ERIC CHEN
vice president / general manager

tel 650.616.7777 / 800.223.4438 x 225
fax 650.616.4800 / 800.223.4428
email ERICCHEN@SPI-HOME.COM

01
7
11
03
Kc⁺
Katalyst
145.1958

31
6
19
20
26
11
Be⁺
Believer
19.010

3

yoga*fuzion*
la jolla

STUDIO
858.459.YOGA f 858.459.9641

5632 la jolla blvd
la jolla, california 92037

www.yogafuzion.com

1
design firm: Willoughby Design Group
art director: Deb Tagtalianidis and
Ann Willoughby
(Creative director)
designer: Lindsay Laricks
client: Kevin Carroll

2
design firm: Helena Seo Design
art director: Helena Seo
designer: Helena Seo
client: SPI Home
software/hardware: Adobe Illustrator
paper/materials: Crane's 134 lb cover,
Pearl White Kid Finish

3
design firm: Miriello Grafico
art director: Dennis Garcia
designer: Sallie Reynolds Allen
client: Yoga Fuzion
software/hardware: Adobe Illustrator
paper/materials: French Smart White 110 lb cover

CANAL
ASSOCIATES LLC

Distinctive City Residences

Mike McCurley
Partner

T   301.343.7331
F   301.215.6453
E   mmccurley@canalassociates.com

7110 Exfair Rd.
Bethesda, MD 20814

www.canalassociates.com

1

2

ROGER ALLEN

Roger Allen Design + Photo
Website: www.rager1.com
E.mail: rager1@mac.com
Vancouver, B.C. Canada
604.738.7696

Motion Picture Advertising

Buddha Jones
1542 Cassil Place
Hollywood, California 90028
johnl@buddhajonestrailers.com
tel 323-962-5100

John Long
Partner

BUD HA JONES

SPIN!™
neapolitan pizza

6541 W. 119th Street   Overland Park, KS 66209
913.451.SPIN   spinpizza.com

GAIL
IOZOFF
816.550.0808

SI GIRA! SI MANGIA! SI PIACE!

1
design firm: Jill Tanenbaum Graphic Design
& Advertising Inc.
designer: Jennifer Prophet
client: Canal Associates LLC
software/hardware: Adobe Illustrator, InDesign,
and Photoshop
paper/materials: Strathmore Natural White
80 lb cover

2
design firm: Rager 1
art director: Roger Allen
designer: Roger Allen
client: Roger Allen
software/hardware: Adobe InDesign
paper/materials: Silk Screen

3
design firm: KBDA
art director: Kim Baer
designer: Keith Knueven
client: Buddha Jones
software/hardware: Adobe Creative Suite

4
design firm: Willoughby Design Group
art director: Deb Tagtalianidis and
Ann Willoughby
(Creative director)
designer: Zack Shubkagel and
Hammerpress
client: SPIN! Neapolitan Pizza

1

NATE QUAN
VP-SALES & OPERATIONS
n.quan@jrne.com

WWW.JOURNEELIGHTING.COM

TELEPHONE 800-886-1880 – FAX 800-886-1881
4607 Lakeview Canyon Rd #500 - Westlake Village, CA 91361

2

3

WE ARE:

Up and Comer™ Apparel for what's big in little! Hip, fresh clothing for ultra cool infants and toddlers.

COURTESY OF:

Lance Hester VICE PRESIDENT

TRACK US DOWN:

12717 West Sunrise Blvd #237
Sunrise, Florida 33323
PH: 954.670.6411 FX: 484.070.6413
EMAIL: lance@up-and-comer.com

WE THINK KIDS ARE:

BORN TO BE GREAT

CHECK US OUT:

up-and-comer.com

4

SOCIALLY AND ENVIRONMENTALLY
CONSCIOUS DESIGN & MARKETING

45-50 30TH ST., 7TH FLOOR
LONG ISLAND CITY, NY 11101

V   718 663 8434
TF 888 224 2204
C   212 721 9764
F   646 224 8375

JULIA@JULIAREICHDESIGN.COM
JULIAREICHDESIGN.COM

JuliaReich
DESIGN

1

design firm: Reactor
art director: Clifton Alexander
designer: Clifton Alexander
client: Journée Lighting
software/hardware: Adobe Illustrator
paper/materials: Endeavor Velvet, embossed

2

design firm: Adlucent
art director: Nicholas Herman
designer: Nicholas Herman
illustrator: Nicholas Herman
client: PriceFight.com
software/hardware: Adobe Illustrator, Mac
paper/materials: 3 color and die-cut on Cougar
Opaque, polyester laser labels

3

design firm: Alphabet Arm Design
designer: Aaron Belyea
client: Up and Comer™
software/hardware: Adobe Illustrator

4

design firm: Julia Reich Design
art director: Julia Reich
designer: Julia Reich
client: Julia Reich Design
software/hardware: Quark Xpress
printing: Terrance Chouinard,
Wells College Book Arts Center

1

2

El
CHILE
Cafe y Cantina

Carlos Rivero
Operator

★

512/457-9900

1809 Manor Rd.
Austin, Texas 78722

3

MINDFUL REVOLUTION

LEIGH-ANNE BROWN
certified yoga instructor & MEd

PHONE: 512-416-8008
LA@mindfulrevolution.com

MINDFULREVOLUTION.COM

4

design firm: Brandfly
art director: Dustin Hassard
designer: Dustin Hassard
client: Bandfly
software/hardware: Adobe Illustrator
paper/materials: Plastic

2

design firm: Zócalo Design
art director: Blake Trabulsi
client: El Chile Cafe y Cantina
software/hardware: Adobe InDesign

3

design firm: The Decoder Ring
Design Concern
art director: Paul Fucik
designer: Paul Fucik
client: Mindful Revolution
software/hardware: Adobe Illustrator
paper/materials: 2/2 color on Cougar Natur
80 lb cover

4

design firm: Judson Design
art director: Jeff Davis
designer: Jeff Davis
client: Davis Guide Service
software/hardware: Adobe CS2
paper/materials: Astrolite, PMS red and bla

1

2

3

David Maloney
Graphic Designer

251 First Avenue North, Suite 400
Minneapolis, Minnesota 55401

Telephone: (612) 372-4612
Facsimile: (612) 372-4617

RedCircleAgency.com
david@RedCircleAgency.com

1

design firm: substance151

art director: Ida Cheinman

designer: Ida Cheinman and Rick Salzman

client: substance151

software/hardware: Adobe Illustrator

paper/materials: Mohawk Navajo, 3/3 colors,
metallic ink

2

design firm: MBA

art director: Mark Brinkman and Mike Coffin

designer: Mark Brinkman and
Caroline Pledger

client: ETI

software/hardware: Adobe Creative Suite

paper/materials: Monadnock Astrolite smooth

3

design firm: Red Circle Agency

art director: David Maloney

designer: David Maloney

client: Red Circle Agency

software/hardware: Adobe Illustrator and InDesign

paper/materials: Hand-set eyelet

1

1

design firm: Zande + Newman Design
art director: Adam Newman
designer: Adam Newman
and Loren Stephens
client: Flavor League

1

2

1

design firm: David Clark Design
art director: David Clark
designer: Becky Gelder
client: Leta Bell
software/hardware: Adobe Illustrator CS
paper/materials: Classic Crest Solar White
80 lb cover
printing: McNally Printing, Tulsa, OK

2

design firm: Crave, Inc.
art director: David Edmundson
designer: Russ Martin
client: Vuru

3

design firm: Foda Studio
art director: Jett Butler
designer: Jett Butler
client: David Hobizal,
Motion Graphics Editor
software/hardware: Adobe Illustrator
paper/materials: 2/1 C2S Satin Laminate

4

design firm: Turnstyle
art director: Ben Graham
designer: Ben Graham
client: Venue
software/hardware: Adobe Illustrator
paper/materials: Mohawk Options
True White 100 lb cover

1

2

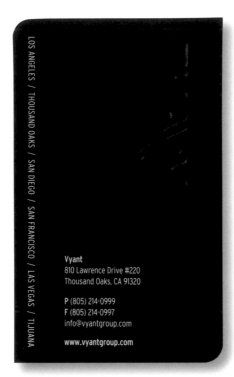

1
design firm: **BR**
art director: **Franklin Oviedo,**
Anthony Magliano

2
design firm: **Vyant Group**
art director: **Dave Carlson**
designer: **Catherine Reisen**

3
design firm: **Dean Johnson Design**
art director: **Scott Johnson**
designer: **Ryan Abegglen**

3

646 MASSACHUSETTS AVENUE
INDIANAPOLIS, INDIANA 46204
T: 317.634.8020
F: 317.634.8054
DEANJOHNSON.COM

SCOTT JOHNSON
SJOHNSON@DEANJOHNSON.COM

MARILYN STRAUSS | FOUNDER

TEL **816** 531.7728
FAX **816** 531.1911

4800 MAIN ST. STE.302
KANSAS CITY, MO 64112

WWW.KCSHAKES.ORG

HEART OF AMERICA
SHAKESPEARE FESTIVAL

ASK@THEDECODERRING.COM
P: 512-933-0079 F: 512-597-1848
WWW.THEDECODERRING.COM

3

4

1

design firm: BR
art director: Nathaniel Cooper
designer: Nathaniel Cooper
client: Heart of America
Shakespeare Festival
software/hardware: Adobe Illustrator, InDesign,
and Photoshop
paper/materials: Spray paint, chipboard

2

design firm: The Decoder Ring
Design Concern
designer: Christian Helms
client: The Decoder Ring
software/hardware: Adobe Illustrator and Photosh
paper/materials: Cougar Opaque

3

design firm: Design Ranch
art director: Michelle Sonderegger
and Ingred Sidie
designer: Tad Carpenter
client: Raeta Estates
software/hardware: Adobe Illustrator

4

design firm: Di Depux
art director: Despina Bournele
designer: Despina Bournele
client: Erato
software/hardware: Adobe Illustrator CS
paper/materials: 1 Pantone, 1 metal Majestic
F098, 250 gsm

MIXOLOGY 101

the
TOM COLLINS

Fill a Collins glass with ice.
You can build this one right
in the glass.

1 oz. Gin
Fill glass with equal amounts:
Sweet & Sour
Soda Water

Garnish with a cherry and
a lime squeeze.

MIXOLOGY 101

the
COSMOPOLITAN

1 1/2 oz. Vodka
1/2 oz. Cointreau or Triple Sec
3/4 oz. Lime Juice

Combine all the ingredients
in a cocktail shaker filled with
ice. Shake well. Strain into a
cocktail glass and garnish with
a lime squeeze.

HILLERY PEREZ

Mixologist

TABC CERTIFIED BARTENDING
FOR SPECIAL EVENTS
AND PRIVATE PARTIES

713 366 2804 CELL
HILLERYPZ.BARTENDER@YAHOO.COM

MIXOLOGY 101

the
SIDECAR

1 1/2 oz. Brandy
1/2 oz. Triple Sec
1/2 oz. Lemon or Lime Juice

Combine all the ingredients
in a shaker filled with ice,
shake well and strain into a
cocktail glass.

MIXOLOGY 101

the
COSMOPOLITAN

1 1/2 oz. Vodka
1/2 oz. Cointreau or Triple Sec
3/4 oz. Lime Juice

Combine all the ingredients
in a cocktail shaker filled with
ice. Shake well. Strain into a
cocktail glass and garnish with
a lime squeeze.

MIXOLOGY 101

the
MANHATTAN

1 1/2 oz. Maker's Mark
Bourbon
1/4 oz. Sweet Vermouth or
Dry Vermouth
dash Angostura Bitters
(optional)

Combine all the ingredients
in a cocktail shaker filled with
ice. Shake well. Strain into a
cocktail glass and garnish
with a cherry.

1

2

3

	1		2		3
design firm:	Sherry Matthews	design firm:	Di Depux	design firm:	Di Depux
art director:	Gretchen Garven Hicks	art director:	Despina Bournele	art director:	Despina Bournele
designer:	Gretchen Garven Hicks	designer:	Despina Bournele	designer:	Despina Bournele
client:	Hillery Perez	client:	Mas abajo/ giannitsas george	client:	Fani Partheniou, architect
software/hardware:	Adobe Illustrator CS	software/hardware:	Adobe Illustrator CS	software/hardware:	Adobe Illustrator CS
paper/materials:	Classic Crest Natural White 110 lb cover	paper/materials:	2 Pantone, Metal velvet 250 gsm	paper/materials:	2 Pantone, metal Zeta 300 gsm

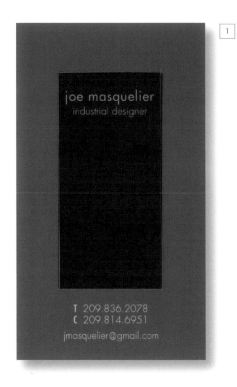

1

design firm: Joe Masquelier Designs
designer: Joe Masquelier
client: Joe Masquelier Designs

joe masquelier
industrial designer

T 209.836.2078
C 209.814.6951
jmasquelier@gmail.com

1

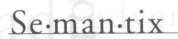

2

3

FEASTS *of* FANCY

PAIGE INMAN catering & event manager

THE HOBBS BUILDING
1427 WEST NINTH STREET · SUITE 103 · KANSAS CITY, MISSOURI 64101
phone 816.841.0166 · www.theweddingcafe.com

STYLISH FOOD & URBAN ELEGANCE

TOBIAS SCHNABEL
GASTGEBER

EBERSTÄDTER STRASSE 7   TELEFON (071 34) 188 55
74182 OBERSULM / SÜLZBACH   TELEFAX (071 34) 91 63 48

WWW.RESTAURANT-ALTER-KLOSTERHOF.DE
INFO@RESTAURANT-ALTER-KLOSTERHOF.DE

ÖFFNUNGSZEITEN   18.00 UHR – 24.00 UHR
DIENSTAG – SAMSTAG   UND NACH VEREINBARUNG

4

1
design firm: Lizette Gecel
designer: Lizette Gecel
client: The Sorrell Company
software/hardware: Adobe Illustrator CS2
paper/materials: Neenah Paper
Eames Furniture

2
design firm: Evenson Design
art director: Stan Evenson
designer: Mark Sojka
client: Semantix Creative
software/hardware: EPS

3
design firm: Bungalow Creative
art director: Christopher Huelshorst
designer: Carrie Kish
client: Feasts of Fancy
software/hardware: Quark Xpress
paper/materials: Carnival Vellum 100 lb cover

4
design firm: Jens Mogler
designer: Jens Mogler
client: Restaurant Alter Klosterhof
software/hardware: Macromedia Freehand
paper/materials: Gmund Blanc Beige Creme

1

ZACK FUENTES
Owner Operator
zfuentes@unclebillysaustin.com

1530 BARTON SPRINGS RD
AUSTIN, TEXAS 78704
unclebillysaustin.com
512.476.0100 TEL
512.476.0104 FAX

SHANE STARK
Owner Operator
sstark@unclebillysaustin.com

1530 BARTON SPRINGS RD
AUSTIN, TEXAS 78704
unclebillysaustin.com
512.476.0100 TEL
512.476.0104 FAX

DARREN HARRELL
General Manager
dharrell@unclebillysaustin.com

1530 BARTON SPRINGS RD
AUSTIN, TEXAS 78704
unclebillysaustin.com
512.476.0100 TEL
512.476.0104 FAX

2

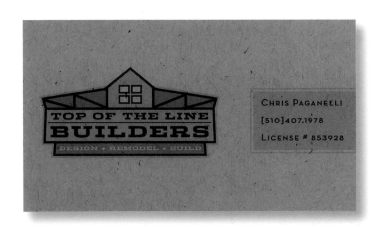

CHRIS PAGANELLI
[510]407.1978
LICENSE # 853928

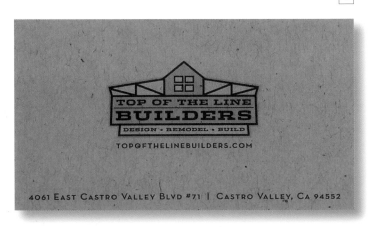

3

1		2		3	
design firm:	Idea 21	design firm:	Miles Design	design firm:	Murillo Design, Inc.
art director:	Tom Berno	art director:	Josh Miles	art director:	Roland Murillo
designer:	Jeff Davis	designer:	Eric Folzenlogel	designer:	Roland Murillo
client:	Uncle Billy's: Brew and Que	client:	Top of the Line Builders	client:	Murillo Design, Inc.
software/hardware:	Adobe CS2	software/hardware:	Adobe Illustrator CS2	paper/materials:	Wood
paper/materials:	Letterpress on coaster stock	paper/materials:	French Kraft 100 lb cover		

1

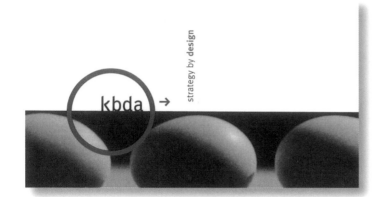

strategy by design

kbda →

(p) 310.287.2400   2558 Overland Avenue
(f) 310.287.0909   Los Angeles, CA 90064
(w) kbda.com

Jamie Cavanaugh
New Media
jamiec@kbda.com

kbda →

2

Ralph Deal
Composer, musician, engineer

161 Leverington Avenue,
Suite 1001,
Philadelphia, PA 19127-2034
215.483.2415 ph 215.483.4554 fx
audio-jack.com

Audio Jack

Purveyors of fine music & sound design

Audio Jack

57TH&IRVING

PRODUCTIONS

TOM GANJAMIE
Director of Development

645 Madison Avenue, Suite 9B
New York, New York 10022
phone: 212-995-0057 *cell:* 908-787-3090
email: tom@57irving.com *web:* www.57irving.com

3

4

marisa estrada
o)323.230.9600 c)323.252.9398 e)info@ritzyperiwinkle.com

ritzyperiwinkle.com

RITZY PERIWINKLE
fade proof design sweetness...

1
design firm: KBDA
art director: Kim Baer
designer: Jamie Diersing
client: KBDA
software/hardware: Adobe

2
design firm: D4 Creative Group
art director: Wicky Lee
client: Audio Jack
software/hardware: Adobe Photoshop
and Quark Xpress
paper/materials: Strathmore Bright White

3
design firm: Matthew Schwartz
Design Studio
art director: Matthew Schwartz
client: 57th and Irving Productions
software/hardware: Adobe Illustrator and InDesign

4
design firm: Ritzy Periwinkle
art director: Marisa Estrada
designer: Marisa Estrada
client: Ritzy Periwinkle
software/hardware: Adobe Illustrator
paper/materials: 2/2 Classic Crest Soft White
Super Smooth

Sean Baker
Senior Designer

Liquid Agency | Brand Marketing

448 S. Market Street
San Jose, CA 95113
T 408.850.8859
M 510.329.7189
E sean@liquidagency.com
W liquidagency.com

Isalda (Izzy) Hermosillo
Accounting Specialist

Liquid Agency | Brand Marketing

448 S. Market Street
San Jose, CA 95113
T 408.850.8839
E izzy@liquidagency.com
W liquidagency.com

Julia Held
Designer

Liquid Agency | Brand Marketing

448 S. Market Street
San Jose, CA 95113
T 408.850.8849
M 408.209.5822
E julia@liquidagency.com
W liquidagency.com

Isalda (Izzy) Hermosillo
Accounting Specialist

Liquid Agency | Brand Marketing

448 S. Market Street
San Jose, CA 95113
T 408.850.8839
E izzy@liquidagency.com
W liquidagency.com

2

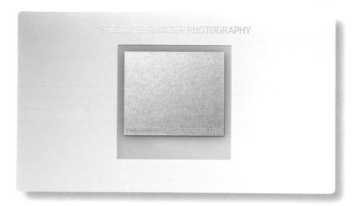

3

Gregory Gersch
Creative Director

eyebeam

Identity · Branding · Marketing

202 518-5888
greg@eyebeamcreative.com

Eyebeam Creative LLC
1545 18th Street NW · Suite 406
Washington DC 20036-1345

1		2		3	
design firm:	Liquid Agency	design firm:	Geyrhalter Design	design firm:	Eyebeam Creative LLC
art director:	Alfredo Muccino	art director:	Fabian Geyrhalter	art director:	Greg Gersch
designer:	Joshua Swanbeck	designer:	Fabian Geyrhalter	designer:	Greg Gersch
client:	Liquid Agency		and Jacqueline Sung	client:	Eyebeam Creative LLC
software/hardware:	Adobe InDesign	client:	Fabian Geyrhalter Photography	software/hardware:	Adobe Illustrator
paper/materials:	Plastic	software/hardware:	Adobe Illustrator		and Quark Xpress
		paper/materials:	Plastic	paper/materials:	Strathmore Ultimate White
					Laid 110 lb cover

DAVID GARRIDO

O's Campus Cafe and Catering
ACES Building
201 East 24th Street 2.234
Austin, Texas 78712-2.234
phone: (512) 232-9060
fax: (512) 232-9097
email: ocafe@mail.aces.utexas.edu
web: www.aces.utexas.edu/ocafe

MONTE·VISTA
CONDOMINIUMS

Roya Johnson · *Broker, CRB*
Coldwell Banker United, Realtors®

6000 Shepherd Mountain Cove · Austin, Texas 78730
phone.512.472.1000 · fax.512.328.1000 · cell.512.585.0334
roya@royanet.com · www.discovermontevista.com

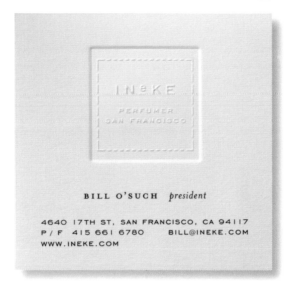

BILL O'SUCH *president*

4640 17TH ST, SAN FRANCISCO, CA 94117
P / F 415 661 6780   BILL@INEKE.COM
WWW.INEKE.COM

Clint Fraser Marketing Director

PO Box 2373, Prince George, BC, Canada V2N 2S6
Telephone: 250.561.0432 ext. 202 Fax: 250.561.0450
clint@nbctourism.com www.northernbctourism.com

1

design firm: Sibley Peteet Design—Austin
art director: Rex Peteet
designer: Rex Peteet
client: O's Campus Cafe
software/hardware: Adobe InDesign
and Quark Xpress
paper/materials: Card stock with fleck

2

design firm: Sibley Peteet Design—Austin
art director: Rex Peteet
designer: Kris Worley
client: Monte Vista Condominiums
software/hardware: Adobe InDesign
and Quark Xpress
paper/materials: Via Felt

3

design firm: Helena Seo Design
art director: Helena Seo
designer: Helena Seo
client: Ineke, LLC
software/hardware: Adobe Illustrator

4

design firm: smashLAB
art director: Eric Karjaluoto
designer: Peter Pimentel
illustrator: Peter Pimentel
client: The Northern BC
Tourism Association
software/hardware: Adobe Illustrator
paper/materials: Cougar Cover 100 lb cover

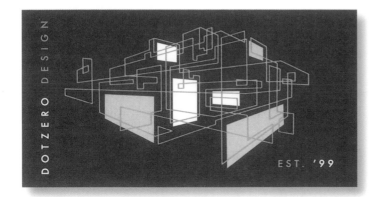

KAREN WIPPICH
208 SW STARK ST, #307 • PORTLAND, OR 97204
tel: 503 892 9262   fax: 503 228 9403
email: karenw@dotzerodesign.com   www.dotzerodesign.com

Karen Wippich karenw@dotzerodesign.com
208 SW Stark St // #307 // Portland, OR 97204
PH: [503] 892 9262 // FX: [503] 228 9403

www.dotzerodesign.com

2

3

1	2	3
design firm: Dotzero Design	design firm: Timber Design Co.	design firm: Blok
designer: Karen Wippich and Jon Wippich	art director: Lars Lawson	art director: Vanessa Eckstein
client: Dotzero Design	client: Timber Design Co.	designer: Vanessa Eckstein
software/hardware: Adobe Illustrator and Photoshop	software/hardware: Freehand and Quark Xpress	client: Bandolero Films

MARTIN DUFFY

martin@johnstonduffy.com   PHONE 215 389 2888   FAX 215 389 2988
803 S⁰4TH STREET First Floor PHILADELPHIA PENNSYLVANIA 191473103

a self service dog wash and pet boutique

Jan Bulawa   2418 B Sunset Blvd.
jan@sashassudsnduds.com   Houston, Texas 77055
                    713.533.1117

www.sashassudsnduds.com

Danette Miller

netteables@netteables.com
4647 E Chandler Blvd Suite #2
Phoenix, AZ 85048
p 480.705.0747 f 480.705.9626

netteables.com

3

4

Rachel Stikeleather
Principal, Creative Director

107 Leland St., Suite 2
Austin, TX 78704

rachel@creativesuitcase.com
office: 512 326 3667
cell: 512 750 6087

creative suitcase

creativesuitcase.com :: packed with ideas

1

design firm: Johnston Duffy
art director: Martin Duffy
designer: Johnston Duffy
client: Johnston Duffy
software/hardware: Adobe Illustrator on MAC
paper/materials: Mohawk Superfine

2

design firm: Limb Design
art director: Linda Limb
designer: Trisha Cano
client: Shasha's Suds n Duds
software/hardware: Adobe InDesign

3

design firm: Campbell Fisher Design
art director: Greg Fisher
designer: Kristy Roehrs
client: Nettables
(delectable accessories)
software/hardware: Adobe Illustrator
paper/materials: Domtar Carrara White
120 lb cover

4

design firm: Creative Suitcase
art director: Rachel Stikeleather
designer: Rachel Stikeleather
client: Creative Suitcase
software/hardware: Quark Xpress
paper/materials: Classic Crest

1

Ghada Ghanem : SOPRANO
telephone **961.3.939141** | ghadaghanem@yahoo.com

telephone **961.3.939141** | ghadaghanem@yahoo.com

2

PÄGLIŪCO

PAGLIUCO DESIGN COMPANY
213 West Institute Place Suite 508 Chicago, Illinois 60610
T/312 943 4281 F/312 943 6946 W/ pagliuco.com

Michael Pagliuco / Principal
michael@pagliuco.com

elma backman
designer
m: elmaback@gmail.com
p: +354. 695 6900

3

4

JAMES SONG
VISUAL DESIGN

415 971 0351
bluntside.com
james@bluntside.com

1

design firm: Mayda Freije Makdessi
art director: Mayda Freije Makdessi
designer: Mayda Freije Makdessi
client: Ghada Ghanem
software/hardware: Adobe Illustrator
and Quark Xpress
paper/materials: uncoated 200 gsm

2

design firm: Pagliuco Design Company
art director: Michael Pagliuco
designer: Michael Pagliuco
client: Pagliuco Design Company
paper/materials: Mohawk Superfine

3

design firm: Nicole Nicolaus
art director: Nicole Nicolaus
designer: Nicole Nicolaus
client: Elma Backman
(fashion designer)
software/hardware: Adobe Illustrator
and InDesign CS2
paper/materials: packaging paper, offset print

4

design firm: James Song
art director: James Song
designer: James Song
illustrator: James Song
client: James Song
software/hardware: Adobe Illustrator
paper/materials: Blind emboss on
110 lb matte paper

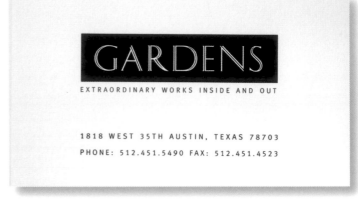

1

1

design firm: Sibley Peteet Design—Austin

art director: Rex Peteet

designer: Mark Brinkman

client: Gardens

software/hardware: Adobe InDesign
and Quark Xpress

paper/materials: Monadnock

2

design firm: Markcom Consulting Group

art director: Mark LeRoy

designer: Mark LeRoy

client: Empress Restaurant

software/hardware: Adobe Illustrator

paper/materials: French Paper, PMS metallic inks

3

design firm: Julie Grantz Design

art director: Julie Grantz

designer: Julie Grantz

client: Julie Grantz Design

software/hardware: Adobe Illustrator CS2

paper/materials: Strathmore Natural 80 lb cover,
letterpress front 2 color,
back blind

2

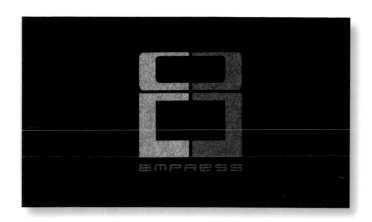

Ardi Entezam

8264 Sunset Boulevard
West Hollywood, California 90046

323-656-8377 T
323-656-8457 F
ardi@empressrestaurant.com
empressrestaurant.com

3

IT IS SIMPLE

LISTEN : SENTIRE

JULIE GRANTZ

87 LINDA AVENUE, PIEDMONT, CA 94611
JULIE@JULIEGRANTZ.COM 510.290.4579

1

design firm: Den Herder Design
art director: Jesse Den Herder
designer: Jesser Den Herder
illustrator: Jesse Den Herder
client: Den Herder Design
software/hardware: Adobe Illustrator CS,
Adobe Photoshop CS

2

design firm: The Decoder Ring
Design Concern
designer: Christian Helms
client: The Outfit Media Group
software/hardware: Adobe Illustrator
paper/materials: Cougar Opaque

3

design firm: Nothing: Something: NY
art director: Kevin Landwehr
designer: Kevin Landwehr
and Devin Becker
client: The Alembic Bar & Restaurant
paper/materials: Neenah Classic Crest
Natural White 130 lb

4

design firm: Nothing: Something: NY
art director: Kevin Landwehr
designer: Kevin Landwehr
and Devin Becker
client: A & G Merch Alhadeff /
Goldhand

1

	1		2		3
design firm:	Bungalow Creative	design firm:	Foda Studio	design firm:	Bungalow Creative
art director:	Christopher Huelshorst	art director:	Jett Butler	art director:	Christopher Huelshorst
designer:	Carrie Kish	designer:	Jett Butler and Trina Bentley	designer:	Carrie Kish
client:	Unicorn Theatre	client:	BWM Group	client:	Fortner Hall Artisan Textiles
software/hardware:	Quark Xpress	software/hardware:	Adobe Illustrator	software/hardware:	Quark Xpress
paper/materials:	Letterpress Chipboard	paper/materials:	1/1 C2S, satin laminate	paper/materials:	Lustro Dull 100 lb cover

2

3

1

2

3

Rex Wilder
President, Chief Creative Officer

JNR8 goodvertising™
15332 Antioch Street, No. 538
Pacific Palisades CA 90272

e. rex@jnr8.com
p. 310.890.2421

1	2	3
design firm: Bungalow Creative	design firm: Hybrid 6 Studios	design firm: dpd studio
art director: Christopher Huelshorst	art director: Scott Allen	art director: Dennis Purcell
designer: Christine Taylor	designer: Scott Allen	designer: Dennis Purcell
client: Bungalow Creative	client: Hybrid 6 Studios	client: JNR8
software/hardware: Quark Xpress	software/hardware: Adobe Photoshop	software/hardware: Adobe Illustrator

Heather Beckel Guntert, Managing Director

I&O Communications

327 Congress, Suite 200   Austin, Texas 78701

heather@iandocom.com   www.iandocom.com

p 512.288.4054   m 512.507.3809

io

1

insight & outreach

io

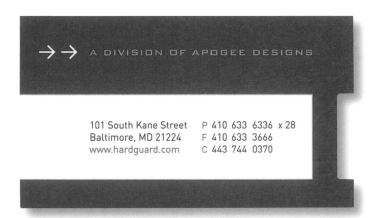

→ → A DIVISION OF APOGEE DESIGNS

101 South Kane Street   P 410 633 6336 x 28
Baltimore, MD 21224   F 410 633 3666
www.hardguard.com   C 443 744 0370

→ **HARDGUARD**®

KEVIN BARNES
VICE PRESIDENT, PRODUCT DEVELOPMENT

kevin.barnes@apogeedesigns.com

2

	1		2		3
design firm:	MBA	design firm:	substance151	design firm:	Reactor
art director:	Mark Brinkman	art director:	Ida Cheinman	art director:	Clifton Alexander
designer:	Caroline Pledger	designer:	Ida Cheinman and Rick Salzman	designer:	Chase Wilson
client:	I&O Communications	client:	HardGuard	client:	Reactor
software/hardware:	Adobe Creative Suite	software/hardware:	Adobe Illustrator	software/hardware:	Adobe Illustrator
paper/materials:	Strathmore Natural White	paper/materials:	Mohawk Navajo, die-cut, 2-sided		

CF-24

Chase Wilson

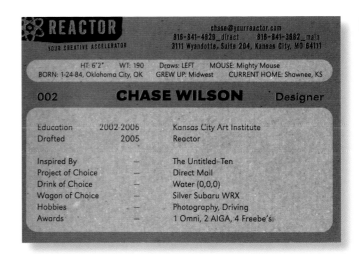

REACTOR
YOUR CREATIVE ACCELERATOR

chase@yourreactor.com
816-841-4929_direct   816-841-3682_main
3111 Wyandotte, Suite 204, Kansas City, MO 64111

| HT: 6'2" | WT: 190 | Draws: LEFT | MOUSE: Mighty Mouse |
| BORN: 1-24-84, Oklahoma City, OK | GREW UP: Midwest | CURRENT HOME: Shawnee, KS | |

002   CHASE WILSON   Designer

Education	2002-2006	Kansas City Art Institute
Drafted	2005	Reactor
Inspired By	—	The Untitled–Ten
Project of Choice	—	Direct Mail
Drink of Choice	—	Water (0,0,0)
Wagon of Choice	—	Silver Subaru WRX
Hobbies	—	Photography, Driving
Awards	—	1 Omni, 2 AIGA, 4 Freebe's

1B-8
REACTOR
Clifton
Alexander

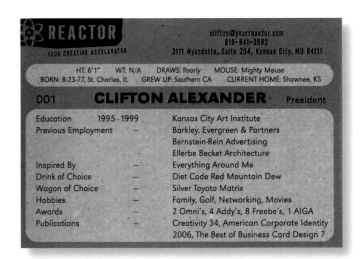

REACTOR
YOUR CREATIVE ACCELERATOR

clifton@yourreactor.com
816-841-3682
3111 Wyandotte, Suite 204, Kansas City, MO 64111

| HT: 6'1" | WT: N/A | DRAWS: Poorly | MOUSE: Mighty Mouse |
| BORN: 8-23-77, St. Charles, IL | GREW UP: Southern CA | CURRENT HOME: Shawnee, KS | |

001   CLIFTON ALEXANDER   President

Education	1995-1999	Kansas City Art Institute
Previous Employment	—	Barkley, Evergreen & Partners
		Bernstein-Rein Advertising
		Ellerbe Becket Architecture
Inspired By	—	Everything Around Me
Drink of Choice	—	Diet Code Red Mountain Dew
Wagon of Choice	—	Silver Toyota Matrix
Hobbies	—	Family, Golf, Networking, Movies
Awards	—	2 Omni's, 4 Addy's, 8 Freebe's, 1 AIGA
Publications	—	Creativity 34, American Corporate Identity
		2006, The Best of Business Card Design 7

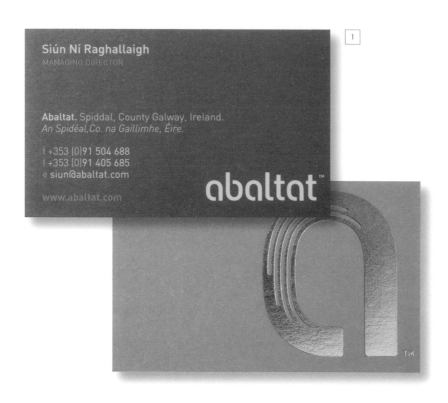

1

Siún Ní Raghallaigh
MANAGING DIRECTOR

Abaltat. Spiddal, County Galway, Ireland.
An Spidéal,Co. na Gaillimhe, Éire.

t +353 (0)91 504 688
f +353 (0)91 405 685
e siun@abaltat.com

www.abaltat.com

abaltat™

2

Jan Šabach
graphic design

326 Degraw Street, Apt. 3
Brooklyn, NY 11231
(646) 220 3226
jansabach@mac.com
www.creativehotlist.com/j-sabach

CHRIS LEARY

225 Broadway
Suite 1670
San Diego CA 92101
tel: 619 435 2458 x5120
fax: 619 365 3026
cleary@ezgds.com
www.ezgds.com

ez **gds**

on demand **travel business solutions**

3

Benjamin Daniels
Writing / Editing Consultant

tag communication services

1227 Pine Street
Philadelphia, PA 19107
T|610.661.3783 C|215.806.8409
benjamin.daniels@sap.com
www.tagcs.com

4

2

3

MARCIA WALDORF
Partner

P.O. BOX 771
52965 CEDAR CREST DRIVE
IDYLLWILD, CA 92549
T. 951.659.2580
F. 951.659.3700
MARCIA@WALDORFCRAWFORD.COM
WALDORFCRAWFORD.COM

4

1

design firm: Lefty Lexington Design
art director: Nate Garn and John Rockwell
designer: Nate Garn and John Rockwell
client: Lefty Lexington Design
software/hardware: Adobe Photoshop
and Quark Xpress
paper/materials: French

2

design firm: The Decoder Ring
Design Concern
designer: Derrit DeRouen
client: DeRouen & Company
software/hardware: Adobe Photoshop
paper/materials: Gmund Sandstone

3

design firm: Evenson Design
art director: Stan Evenson
designer: Mark Sojka
client: Waldorf Crawford
software/hardware: EPS

4

design firm: Boxwood Press
art director: Cheryl L. Clark
designer: Cheryl L. Clark
illustrator: Cheryl L. Clark
client: Boxwood Press
paper/materials: Rives BFK

1

3

1

design firm: Design Ranch
art director: Michelle Sonderegger
and Ingred Sidie
designer: Michelle Sonderegger
and Ingred Sidie
client: Bluebird Cafe
software/hardware: Adobe Illustrator

2

design firm: MBA
designer: Mark Brinkman
and Caroline Pledger
illustrator: Chris Gall
client: Hill Country Weavers
software/hardware: Adobe Creative Suite
paper/materials: Strathmore Natural White

3

design firm: The Decoder Ring
Design Concern
art director: Paul Fucik
designer: Paul Fucik
client: Rosehip Flora
software/hardware: Adobe Illustrator and Photoshop
paper/materials: 1/1 color screenprint,
French Arctic Ice 80 lb cover

1

AVENELLE ARCHILLE

Belles Pralines

new orleans, louisiana
PHONE 504.952.2631
WEB www.bellespralines.com

2

rodrigo fernandez
915.892.3357 | rfs@sotoa.com

500 W. Overland El Paso, Texas 79901

1

design firm: Creative Zumo
art director: Christy Hackenberg
and Gaby Tillero
designer: Christy Hackenberg
and Gaby Tillero
client: Belles Pralines
software/hardware: Adobe Illustrator and InDesign
paper/materials: Classic Crest Solar White 130 lb cover

2

design firm: Joel Martinez
designer: Joel Martinez
client: Sotoa Office Building
software/hardware: Adobe Illustrator CS2
paper/materials: Classic Crest 80 lb cover,
printing: embossed logo,
PMS 138 and 181

3

design firm: Bakken Creative Co.
art director: Michelle Bakken
designer: Gina Mondello, Tae Hatayama
client: Bakken Creative Co.
software/hardware: Adobe Illustrator

1

PRISM

Jon K. Rodgers
Principal

Prism Development Company
625 N Michigan Avenue Suite 500
Chicago Illinois 60611
P 312 782 6700
F 312 782 6401
j.rodgers@prismcompany.com
prismcompany.com

2

SUSAN SMELTZER

ESTEEMED CONCERT PIANIST, COMPOSER, AND TEACHER
extraordinaire of over 25 years: US representative to the
Second Van Cliburn International Piano Competition
and recipient of the 1969 Fulbright Scholarship to
Vienna ❧ PRIVATE LESSONS for students of *all ages*

713 991 4945

8102 Tavenor Lane, Houston, Texas 77075

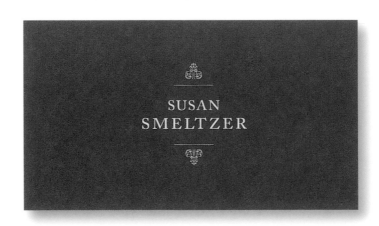

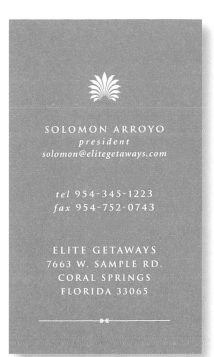

SOLOMON ARROYO
president
solomon@elitegetaways.com

tel 954-345-1223
fax 954-752-0743

ELITE GETAWAYS
7663 W. SAMPLE RD.
CORAL SPRINGS
FLORIDA 33065

ELITE GETAWAYS

954-345-1223

WWW.ELITEGETAWAYS.COM

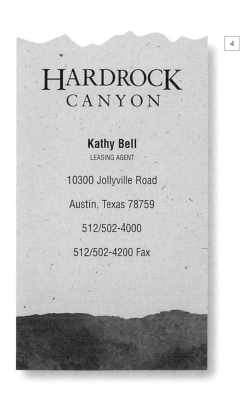

HARDROCK
CANYON

Kathy Bell
LEASING AGENT

10300 Jollyville Road

Austin, Texas 78759

512/502-4000

512/502-4200 Fax

3

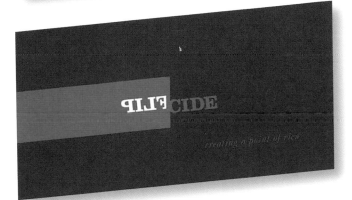

1

design firm: Subplot Design, Inc.
art director: Matthew Clark and Roy White
designer: Matthew Clark and Roy White
client: Subplot Design, Inc.
software/hardware: Adobe Illustrator

2

design firm: Swirl
designer: Carlos R. Zapata
client: Swirl
software/hardware: Adobe Illustrator
and InDesign CS2

3

design firm: Flipcide
art director: Roy Dequina
designer: Roy Dequina and Pavla Diab
client: Flipcide
software/hardware: Adobe Illustrator

1

2

3

SINK IT

Terry McLaughlin President
3256 Karley Crescent, Coquitlam, BC, Canada V3E3E9
t: (866) 255-0694 f: (604) 552-2898 terry@justsinkit.com

First aid for your putting

4

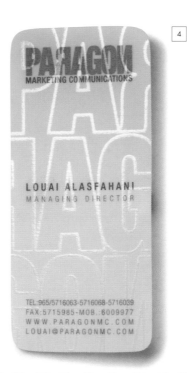

PARAGON
MARKETING COMMUNICATIONS

LOUAI ALASFAHANI
MANAGING DIRECTOR

TEL:965/5716063-5716068-5716039
FAX:5715985-MOB.:6009977
WWW.PARAGONMC.COM
LOUAI@PARAGONMC.COM

1

design firm: Zande + Newman Design
art director: Adam Newman
designer: Adam Newman
client: The Savvy Gourmet
software/hardware: Adobe Illustrator
paper/materials: French Durotone

2

design firm: Liska + Associates
art director: Steve Liska
designer: Tantika Tivorat
client: Brad Lynch
software/hardware: Adobe InDesign and Illustrator
paper/materials: Crane's Kid Finish
Flourescent White 170 lb cover

3

design firm: smashLAB
art director: Eric Karjaluoto
designer: Peter Pimentel
client: Sinkit
software/hardware: Adobe Illustrator
paper/materials: Glama clear cover

4

design firm: Paragon Marketing
Communications
art director: Louai Alasfahani
designer: Khalid Al-Rifae
client: Paragon Marketing
Communications
software/hardware: Adobe Illustrator
paper/materials: Fedrigoni 20 gsm

1

2

1	**2**	**3**
design firm: **Sheriff Design**	design firm: **CDI Studios**	design firm: **Briedis**
art director: **Paul Sheriff**	art director: **Brian Felgar**	art director: **Ruuta Birina**
designer: **Paul Sheriff**	designer: **Tracy Casstevens**	designer: **Ruuta Birina**
client: **Towers and Turrets**	client: **Three Square**	client: **R.B. Bairin**
software/hardware: **Quark Xpress**	software/hardware: **Adobe Illustrator**	software/hardware: **Adobe Illustrator CS2**
	paper/materials: **Neenah Environment**	paper/materials: **Packing paper**

3

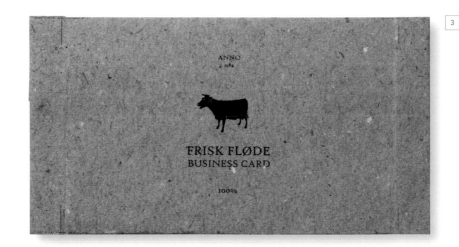

R.B.Bairin

+ 371 639 46 47
bairin[at]gmail.com
ruutabirina

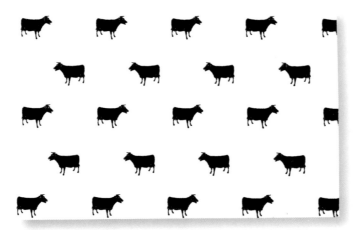

1

2

3

Bill Zbaren
photographer

Z**B**AREN

2232 West Giddings Street
Chicago, Illinois 60625
773 218 9395
bz@zbaren.com

4

705, RUE GOHIER, MONTRÉAL (QUÉBEC) H4L 3H9
514.744.6311
DOMINIQUE@LAMBERTCOMMUNICATIONS.COM
WWW.LAMBERTCOMMUNICATIONS.COM

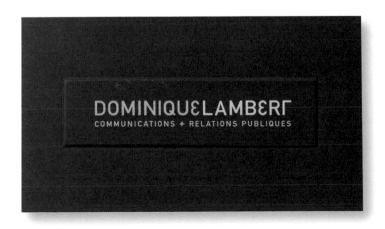

DOMINIQU**E**LAMBER**T**
COMMUNICATIONS + RELATIONS PUBLIQUES

1

design firm: Miles Design
art director: Josh Miles
designer: Eric Folzenlogel
client: Novia
software/hardware: Adobe Illustrator CS
paper/materials: 100 lb cover, offset, emboss

2

design firm: MBA
art director: Mark Brinkman
designer: Caroline Pledger
client: Yield
software/hardware: Adobe Creative Suite
paper/materials: Strathmore Platinum White

3

design firm: Liska + Associates
art director: Steve Liska
designer: Vanessa Oltmanns
client: Bill Zbaren
software/hardware: Adobe InDesign and Illustrator
paper/materials: Mohawk Superfine 130 lb cover

4

design firm: Philippe Archontakis
art director: Philippe Archontakis
client: Dominique Lambert
software/hardware: Adobe Illustrator on MAC
paper/materials: 2 PMS, Emboss, Mohawk White

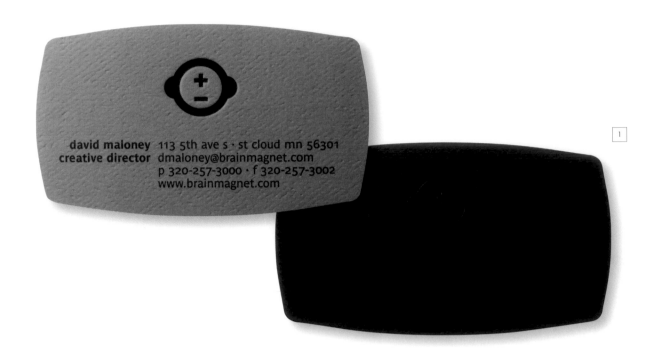

david maloney   113 5th ave s · st cloud mn 56301
creative director   dmaloney@brainmagnet.com
                     p 320-257-3000 · f 320-257-3002
                     www.brainmagnet.com

Jean Tardif
ARCHITECTE

T 514.578.9359
jtardif@btae.ca

bt
bt architecture-energie
www.btae.ca

1

design firm: Brain Magnet

art director: David Maloney

client: Brain Magnet

software/hardware: Adobe Illustrator and InDesign

2

design firm: Philippe Archontakis

art director: Philippe Archontakis

designer: Philippe Archontakis

client: Alexandre Blouin BT Architects

software/hardware: Mac—Adobe Illustrator

paper/materials: Mohawk, 1 PMS and Emboss

3

design firm: Steinzeit-mediendesign

art director: Peggy Stein

designer: Peggy Stein

client: Steinzeit-mediendesign

software/hardware: Adobe Illustrator and InDesign

paper/materials: Evergreen, 220 gsm

3

steinzeit-mediendesign   Ottweilerstraße 26a   Fon: +49 211.48 46 84-0
D-40476 Düsseldorf   Fax: +49 211.48 46 84-26

mail@steinzeit-mediendesign.de

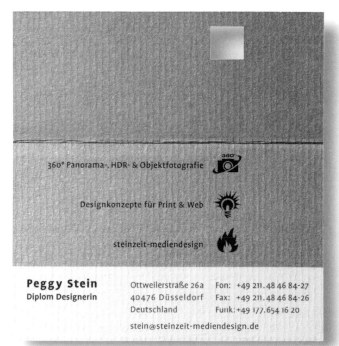

360° Panorama-, HDR- & Objektfotografie

Designkonzepte für Print & Web

steinzeit-mediendesign

Peggy Stein   Ottweilerstraße 26a   Fon: +49 211.48 46 84-27
Diplom Designerin   40476 Düsseldorf   Fax: +49 211.48 46 84-26
Deutschland   Funk:+49 177.654 16 20

stein@steinzeit-mediendesign.de

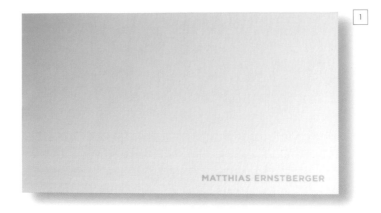

1

MATTHIAS ERNSTBERGER

Matthias@ Sagmeister.com
222 West 14th Street, Suite 15A
New York City, NY 10011
T 212·647 1789 F 212·647 1788
www.Sagmeister.com

SAGMEISTER INC

ISTER INC.

Matthias@ Sagmeister.com
222 West 14th Street, Suite 15A
New York City, NY 10011
T 212·647 1789 F 212·647 1788
www.Sagmeister.com

1

design firm: Sagmeister Inc.
art director: Stefan Sagmeister
designer: Matthias Ernstberger

Matthias@ Sagmeister.com
222 West 14th Street, Suite 15A
New York City, NY 10011
T 212·647 1789 F 212·647 1788
www.Sagmeister.com

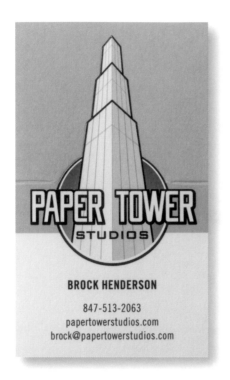

1

2

3

Jamie Gibbs – Director

Limited Fashion, 54 Bury Old Road,
Whitefield, Manchester, M45 6TL

Mob: 07739 710899   Tel: 0161 773 1038
Website: www.limitedfashion.co.uk
E-mail: jamie@limitedfashion.co.uk

LIMITED
FASHION

4

SANDRA FRÆNKEL

CONSULTING   INNOVATIONSMANAGERIN/IHK
COACHING   YORCKSTRASSE 22 65195 WIESBADEN
COMMUNICATION   T 06 11-24 00 944   M 01 51-14 70 48 53
                    SF@SANDRA-FRAENKEL.COM

SANDRA FRÆNKEL

1

design firm: Paper Tower Studios
art director: Brock Henderson
designer: Brenden Jones
illustrator: Brenden Jones
client: Paper Tower Studios
software/hardware: Adobe Illustrator
paper/materials: Classic Crest Solar White
100 lb cover

2

design firm: Element
art director: Megan Graham
designer: Megan Graham
client: Draw Productions
software/hardware: Adobe InDesign

3

design firm: Creative Spark
art director: Neil Marra
designer: Andy Mallalieu
client: Limited Fashion
software/hardware: Adobe Illustrator
paper/materials: 300 gsm, matte laminated,
spot varnished, day-glow pink

4

design firm: R975
art director: Marcel Kummerer
designer: Marcel Kummerer
client: Sandra Fraenkel
paper/materials: Splendorgel

1

consulting + development
for creative service firms

pound
interactive

jeremy pound
jeremy@poundi.com

6463 la costa drive # 604
boca raton florida 33433
561.367.8704
www.poundi.com

2

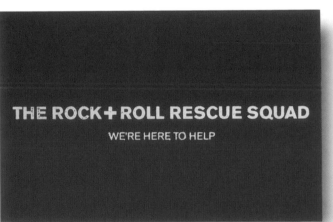

THE ROCK+ROLL RESCUE SQUAD

WE'RE HERE TO HELP

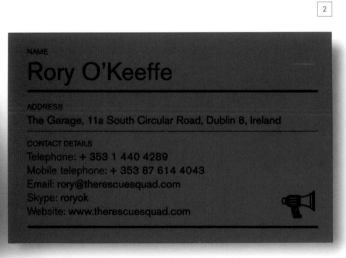

NAME
Rory O'Keeffe

ADDRESS
The Garage, 11a South Circular Road, Dublin 8, Ireland

CONTACT DETAILS
Telephone: + 353 1 440 4289
Mobile telephone: + 353 87 614 4043
Email: rory@therescuesquad.com
Skype: roryok
Website: www.therescuesquad.com

3

FRESH OIL

DESIGN

dan
stebbings
principal

251 Cottage St Pawtucket RI 02860
P 401 709 4656 F 401 709 4655
freshoil.com nelson@freshoil.com

FRESH OIL

1

design firm: Crave, Inc.
art director: David Edmundson
designer: Leo Diaz

2

design firm: Detail Design Studio
art director: Detail Design Studio
designer: Detail Design Studio

3

design firm: Fresh Oil
art director: Dan Stebbings
designer: Dan Stebbings

3

Marcus Engström
Art Direction, Illustration and Graphic Design

■ **MOBILE:** +46 (0)70-424 65 13 **E-MAIL:** MAIL@MARCUSENGSTROM.COM **INTERNET:** WWW.MARCUSENGSTROM.COM ■

4

!nhance
I N H A N C E . N E T

BRANDON HANCE
Founder / Chief Executive Officer

15912 Arminta Street, Van Nuys, CA 91406
email: Brandon.Hance@Inhance.Net
office: 818.455.4340 ext. 224   cell: 818.795.9507
fax: 818.455.4345   toll free: 866.861.9045

1

design firm: Dotzero Design
designer: Karen Wippich and Jon Wippich
client: Unicru
software/hardware: Adobe Illustrator
paper/materials: Classic Crest

2

design firm: Johnston Duffy
art director: Martin Duffy
designer: Andy Evans
client: Wonderboy Clothing
software/hardware: Adobe Illustrator on MAC
paper/materials: 2 color and clear thermal

3

design firm: Marcus Engström
art director: Marcus Engström
designer: Marcus Engström
client: Marcus Engström
software/hardware: Adobe Illustrator
paper/materials: Matte laminate and
spot UV-varnish on one side

4

design firm: Geyrhalter Design
art director: Fabian Geyrhalter
designer: Evelyn Kim
client: Inhance
software/hardware: Adobe Illustrator
paper/materials: Plastic

1

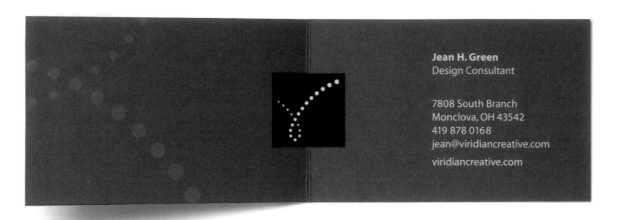

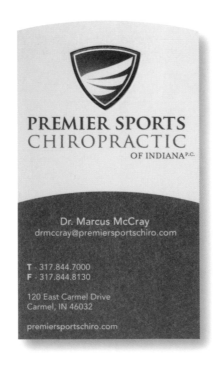

2

```
_MIKE SLACK---------x
///(                )xx
MIKE-SLACK.COM
643 N. MALTMAN AVENUE #106
/// LOS ANGELES >
CA 90026 USA /#213-949-0921
///008017019700///////
```

4

LOU POGORELC
Senior Consultant, Applications

ph 440-365-1864
fx 440-365-1874
cl 440-320-6399

loup@lcgtech.com

DEFINE > DESIGN > DELIVER

LCG TECHNOLOGIES CORPORATION

276 South Logan Street
Elyria, Ohio 44035
www.lcgtech.com

design firm: Viridian
art director: Jean H. Green
client: Viridian

design firm: Miles Design
art director: Josh Miles
designer: Eric Folzenlogel
client: Premier Sports Chiropractic
of Indiana
software/hardware: Adobe Illustrator CS2
paper/materials: 100 lb cover, offset, foil emboss

design firm: Funnel: Eric Kass: Utilitarian +
Commercial + Fine: Art
designer: Eric Kass
client: Mike Slack
software/hardware: Adobe Illustrator CS
paper/materials: Thick uncoated paper
printing: Letterpress

design firm: substance151
art director: Ida Cheinman
designer: Ida Cheinman and Rick Salzman
client: LCG Technologies
software/hardware: Adobe Illustrator
paper/materials: Mohawk Navajo, 2-sided, die-cut

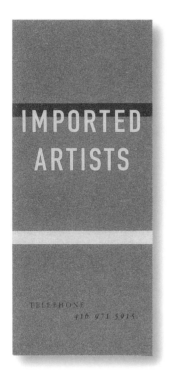

IMPORTED ARTISTS

TELEPHONE
416 971 5915

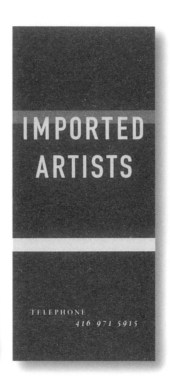

IMPORTED ARTISTS

TELEPHONE
416 971 5915

subject: ALLAN, SUZANNE

address: 49 spadina avenue

suite 100 toronto on canada

M5V 2J1 *fax*: 416 971 7925

www.importedartists.com

suzanne@importedartists.com

IMPORTED ARTISTS

TELEPHONE
416 971 5915

IMPORTED ARTISTS

TELEPHONE
416 971 5915

1

shannon@shannonforsell.com

DECO
RECORDS

Indianapolis Ind. United States of America
©06 Shannon Forsell

SWING'N SING'N!

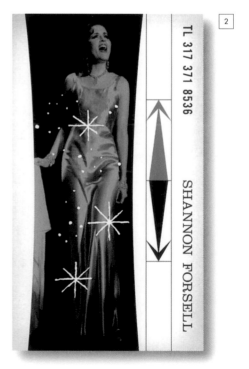

2

TL 317 371 8536

SHANNON FORSELL

3

Carl Churan ENVISIONER ↳

Post Office Box 195, San Ignacio, Cayo District, Belize

U.S. PHONE: 970.485.3865 BELIZE PHONE: 011.501.622.3420

WEB: cyanbelize.com EMAIL: cchuran@cyanbelize.com

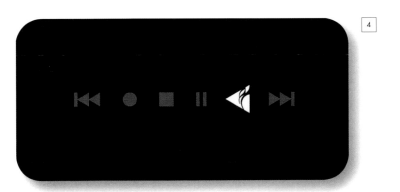

4

◄◄ PRODUCER/ENGINEER

DONNIE BOUTWELL

▶ WWW.THEPARKSTUDIO.COM

The Park {a recording studio}

▶▶ **615:251:4702**

1

design firm: Blok

art director: Vanessa Eckstein

designer: Vanessa Eckstein
and Frances Chen

client: Imported Artists

software/hardware: Adobe Illustrator

paper/materials: Fox River

2

design firm: Funnel: Eric Kass: Utilitarian
Commercial + Fine: Art

art director: Eric Kass

designer: Eric Kass

client: Shannon Forsell

software/hardware: Adobe Illustrator CS

paper/materials: Process offset on coated
white cover with film laminat

3

design firm: 3

writer: Sam Maclay

designer: Tim McGrath

illustrator: Tim McGrath

client: Cyan Belize

software/hardware: Quark Xpress
and Adobe Illustrator

paper/materials: French Paper, letterpress

4

design firm: Foda Studio

art director: Jett Butler

designer: Jett Butler

client: Donnie Boutwell,
Producer/Engineer (music)

software/hardware: Adobe Illustrator

paper/materials: 2/2 Satin laminate

1		2		3	
design firm:	Steinzeit-mediendesign	design firm:	Philippe Archontakis	design firm:	There
art director:	Peggy Stein	art director:	Philippe Archontakis	art director:	There
designer:	Peggy Stein	client:	Frantz Cator	designer:	There
client:	Steinzeit-mediendesign	software/hardware:	Adobe Illustrator on MAC	client:	Downton & Dyer
software/hardware:	Adobe Illustrator	paper/materials:	Neenah, 1 PMS	software/hardware:	Adobe Illustrator
			and foil stamp	paper/materials:	Various

2

2266 Parthenais, loft 306
Montreal (Quebec) H2K 3T5
T 514.598.8181
F 514.379.5959

agence@communi-cator.com
www.communi-cator.com

IDEAS GENERATOR

COMMUNICATOR

3

Downton&Dyer Food Provider since 1878

51-53 Bourke Road Alexandria NSW 2015 Australia
T+61 2 8339 1344 F+61 2 8339 1345 M 0425 796 166
sam.choker@downtonanddyer.com.au
www.downtonanddyer.com.au

Sam Choker
Managing Director

d&d

Color Cubic
2211 NW Front Avenue, Suite 302-E
Portland, OR 97209, USA
T: 971-832-1347
Colorcubic.com
(74)

Counterpart Communication Design
40 South Idlewild
Memphis, TN 38104, USA
T: 901-323-4900   F: 901-578-7878
Counterpartcd.com
(80)

Crave, Inc.
3100 NW Boca Raton Boulevard, Suite 109
Boca Raton, FL 33431, USA
T: 561-417-0780   F: 561-417-0490
Cravebrands.com
(49, 64, 164, 224)

Creative Spark
116 Bury New Road
Whitefield, Manchester M45 6AD,
England
T: 44-0-161-766-1331   F: 44-0-161-766-1441
Creativespark.co.uk
(135, 140, 223)

Creative Suitcase
107 Leland Street, Suite 2
Austin, TX 78704, USA
T: 512-326-3667   F: 512-326-3671
creativesuitcase.com
(187)

Creative Zumo
5030 South Liberty Street
New Orleans, LA 70115, USA
T: 504.304.9887   F: 504.895.8785
(206)

D

D4 Creative Group
161 Leverington Avenue, Suite 1001
Philadelphia, PA 19127, USA
T: 215-483-4555   F: 215-483-4554
D4creative.com
(178)

David Clark Design
1305 E 15th Street, Suite 202
Tulsa, OK 74120, USA
T: 918-295-0044   F: 918-295-0055
Davidclarkdesign.com
(62, 91, 164)

Dean Johnson Design
646 Massachusetts Avenue
Indianapolis, IN 46204, USA
T: 317-634-8020   F: 317-634-8054
Deanjohnson.com
(167)

Den Herder Design
P.O. Box 324
Central Lake, MI 49622, USA
T: 231-590-3583
(192)

Design Center, Ltd.
Knfzova 30
1000 Ljubijana, Slovenia
T: 386-1-519-5072   F: 386-1-519-5072
Cehovin.com
(138)

Design Ranch
1600 Summit
Kansas City, MO 64108, USA
T: 816-472-8668   F: 816-472-8778
Design-ranch.com
(11, 48, 66, 132, 146, 169, 204)

Design Religion
Hampton Court
Rainbow Hill
Worcester, WR3 8NF, England
T: 44-0-1905-724-707
F: 44-0-1905-724-768
Designreligion.co.uk
(97)

Detail Design Studio
11 The Friary
Bow Street
Smithfield, Dublin 7, Ireland
T: 353-1-878-3168   F: 353-1-878-3169
Detail.ie
(91, 151, 200, 224)

Di Depux
4, Eratous Street
Dafni-Athens 172-35, Greece
T: 30-210-9755850   F: 30-210-9751603
Depux.com
(34, 35, 76, 77, 109, 169, 171)

Dossier Creative, Inc.
#402-611 Alexander Street
Vancouver, BC V6A 1E1, Canada
T: 604-255-2097   F: 604-255-2097
Dossiercreative.com
(45, 67, 145)

Dot 1 Design
40 A Corporation Road
Cardiff, South Glamorgan CF11 7AW
South Wales, UK
T: 44-0-78-11-61-6123
Dot1design.co.uk
(129)

Dottie Zimmerman,
Maryville University student
7213 Balson Avenue, Apt 1F
St Louis, MO 63130, USA
T: 314-610-1562
Dottie.zimmerman@gmail.com
(33)

Dotzero Design
208 SW Stark Street, #307
Portland, OR 97204, USA
T: 503-892-9262
Dotzerodesign.com
(69, 99, 121, 184, 226)

dpd studio
408 E 1st Street, Suite 206
Long Beach, CA 90802, USA
T: 310-328-2350   F: 562-495-7101
dpdstudio.com
(107, 197)

E

Element
3292-C North High Street
Columbus, OH 43202, USA
T: 614-447-0906   F: 614-447-1417
Elementville.com
(17, 45, 84, 101, 222)

Elevator
Bana Berislavica
Split 21000, Croatia
T: 098-434-556   F: 021-332-801
Elevator.hr
(151)

Emergent Properties
Fifth Avenue Court
99 5th Avenue, Suite 249
Ottawa Ontario K1S 5P5, Canada
T: 800-521-2715   F: 800-475-2724
Emergentproperties.ca
(24)

Entermotion Design Studios
105 S Broadway
Wichita, KS 67202, USA
T: 316-264-2277   F: 316-264-2274
Entermotion.com
(17, 28, 29, 133, 144)

EPOS, Inc.
1639 16th Street
Santa Monica, CA 90404, USA
T: 310-581-2418   F: 310-581-2422
Eposinc.com
(73)

Evenson Design
4445 Overland
Culver City, CA 90230, USA
T: 310-204-1995   F: 310-204-4879
Evensondesign.com
(32, 88, 174, 203)

Eyebeam Creative LLC
1545 18th Street NW, Suite 406
Washington, D.C. 20036, USA
T: 202-518-5888   F: 202-521-1817
Eyebeamcreative.com
(181)

F

Fangman Design
107 Leland Street, Suite 2
Austin, Texas 78704, USA
T: 512-326-3676   F: 512-326-3671
Fangmandesign.com
(34, 98)

Firebelly Design
2701 W Thomas, 2nd Floor
Chicago, IL 60622, USA
T: 773-489-3200   F: 773-489-3439
Firebellydesign.com
(72)

Flipcide
3751 Robertson Boulevard
Culver City, CA 90232, USA
T: 310-559-3547, x 310   F: 310-559-9137
Flipcide.com
(115, 211)

Foda Studio
1100 W 6th, Suite B
Austin, TX 78703, USA
T: 512-615-2776   F: 512-494-0900
Fodastudio.com
(104, 165, 195, 231)

Folk Creative Ltd.
24 Luke Street
London EC2A 4NT, England
T: 44 (0) 207-739-8444
F: 44 (0) 207-033-0018
Folk.uk.com
(98)

ABOUT THE AUTHOR

Rex Peteet is founding partner and principal designer of Sibley/Peteet, in Austin, Texas. The firm specializes in corporate communications and comprehensive design strategies for clients such as the Sid Richardson Museum, Tivoli/IBM, AMD, GSD&M, Temple-Inland, Haggar Apparel, Mary Kay Cosmetics,Farah/Savane, Milton Bradley (including Scattergories andGuesstures), Dave & Buster's, Brinker International (including Romano's Macaroni Grill and Chili's), Mr. Gatti's Pizza, and Fuddruckers.

Peteet has won numerous regional and national design awards including the New York Art Directors Show, the Los Angeles Art Directors Show, and AR100 and has had several works selected for the permanent collection of the Library of Congress. He has been widely published and featured in many industry magazines and annuals including *Communication Arts*, *Print*, *AIGA*, *Graphis*, *Step*, and *HOW*. In 2005, Peteet was the recipient of the Dallas Society of Visual Communications' highest honor and career achievement award, The Golden Egg. Peteet is also a founding member of the first Texas chapter of AIGA and currently sits on the Advisory Board of AIGA Austin.